PRAISE FOR *Sacred Space*

"In a world in which we are often driven by distractions demanding endlessly our attention and energy, our connection to that which is sacred is often threatened, leaving many of us aching to be held in spaces that support the fulfillment of the deepest calling of our truest selves. With her characteristic honesty, creativity and clarity, Jill Angelo gently engages you in the process of creating that elemental, personalized space, where the sacred may speak to you, in both the solitude and beauty that you can foster by engaging in the steps offered within this gorgeous book. Not only does Jill guide you in the development of a home where the sacred holds you, but also in the making of a path back to yourself again and again. For anyone searching for an increased sense of solace and guidance, this book is simply essential."

—Dora E. McQuaid, author of The Scorched Earth

"This is the best book I have read on creating sacred space. It is both stunningly simple and profound. Anyone, whatever their income or spiritual persuasion, or lack of it, will derive huge and immediate benefit from it. I will give it with joy to all my friends."

—Andrew Harvey, author of The Hope: A Guide to Sacred Activism and Radical Passion

"Turning one's home into a personal sanctuary is a profound act of self-care. This lovely book is a guide to doing that, teaching how to create a place of peace in a world that too often lacks it. Peace begins at home, first in our hearts, then in our personal environment, and then out into the world. Jill Angelo is a marvelous guide to turning anyone's home into a sanctuary for the soul. This little book can help change the world."

—Marianne Williamson, New York Times bestselling author, Return to Love

D1564689

Sacred Space

Sacred Space

TURNING YOUR HOME INTO A SANCTUARY

Jill Angelo

KION YAMAGUCHI PRESS

IMPRINT OF TAYEN LANE

SAN FRANCISCO

MONTREAL

WWW.TAYENLANE.COM

Copyright

Edited by Hollen Reischer
Cover Photographs courtesy Shutterstock
Cover Design Tayen Lane Publishing

For Andrew

Thank you for the push.

Table of Contents

Sacred Space

Foreword

I first met Jill Angelo eight years ago. I was looking for an executive director for the Institute of Sacred Activism and knew at once she would be ideal. I was struck by her beauty, force, focus, passion for life and the no-nonsense groundedness of her spirituality. A wonderful working relationship and deep friendship followed which has changed both of our lives.

During that first meeting, Jill shared the beginnings of her vision of "sacred space" that she has so vividly laid out in this book. I remember saying "'Jill, you have an important message and an original one—you must write a book." She stared at me as if I'd gone crazy. "Me write? No way. You do the writing: I'll do the organizing." I wasn't to be put off. I continued to press her in both subtle and unsubtle ways. Eventually—partly to shut me up, I think—she gave in. The superb and wise result, you hold in your hands.

I responded so powerfully to Jill's initial expression of her vision because I know from experience how empowering and inspiring it can be to consciously create and live in sacred space. For forty years now, all the places I have lived in I have converted into ramshackle and funky temples. My home now, a small cabin in Arkansas, is covered with worn Turkish, Kashmiri and Moroccan prayer rugs. Aboriginal paintings of Uluru and images of Ramana Maharshi, The Black Madonna, and the glorious white lions of Timbavati stare at me and encourage me from the cabin's wood walls. Statues of Rumi, Buddha, Shiva, Mary and Jesus transform flat surfaces into altars. What may seem like chaos to others (one friend describes my decorating style as "Marrakesh meets Benares meets Paris flea market meets a tornado") is, for me, carefully organized in related objects and patterned dances of significance that evoke the aspects of the artistic and mystical traditions I love. Wherever I turn, I am reminded of what exalts my mind, fires my heart and inspires my soul. When I return exhausted from the travels my work demands, I immediately feel restored by the peace and vibrant joy that await me, distilled and enhanced by absence.

Jill's taste—and yours too, probably—is far less baroque than mine, but her love for the sacred in all its forms is no less intense. She knows, as deeply as I do, how essential it is in our chaotic, desacralized, violent world to make of the place where you live a sanctuary, a "sacred space" which will always feed you joy, energy and calm and remind you constantly and gracefully of your deepest values and aspirations. In this increasingly dark age, inspiration of every kind is the oxygen of soul—survival, inspiration and charity begin at home.

What I love and admire most about Jill's vision and this book is its inspired, down-home, practical guidance that anyone, whatever their spiritual path or income level, can immediately apply. Read and study this book and let its simple principles awaken your own "sacred space," and your home will become a sacred space that will sustain you with beauty and celebration of the Divine, and give you courage for your work in the world.

Andrew Harvey
Author, *The Hope: A Guide to Sacred Activism*

JILL ANGELO

PART 1

Your Space

Sacred space is where you can find yourself again and again.

—*Joseph Campbell*

JILL ANGELO

Introduction

And the day came when the risk it took to remain tight in a bud was more painful than the risk it took to blossom.

—Anaïs Nin

The book you are holding is a testament to the fact that you never know just where your life is going to take you, that heaven's path for you is seldom easy. But if you give yourself enough time and you pay attention to the nudges you get along the way, you can see how it all fits together, how both your good and bad experiences have opened doors for you and how heaven has put people in your path all along the way to help you see and hear what's important in life.

I never dreamed as a college student that I would be where I am now, twenty years later. I was hard at work on a degree in Nuclear Medicine, with clinicals in front of me, when something in my gut told me that medicine was not a good choice after all. On a whim, I answered a classified ad for a general office job at a fast-growing company in my native Chicago. Within days, I had started down this new path, working for a small family-owned business in a niche manufacturing industry. I wore multiple hats, as do many in small businesses, and I flourished. The more I could take on, the happier I was.

I quickly threw myself into learning all about the business. As I grew with the company and it thrived, I was flying high, pulling in great income and being told that I was the heartbeat of the company. Heady stuff—a feast for my very left-brained self.

I had also met an IT genius named Richard, who played in a rock band on the weekends. I didn't think life could possibly get any better. Our relationship was energetic, passionate and, like most relationships, had its occasional storms. After five years, we both knew where we wanted our lives to go. Time to buy a house, get married, have kids, add in some more dogs, and live the American dream together.

And we almost did just that.

There was a house I'd passed many times over the years. It had something special about it, a charm I adored. So when a For Sale sign suddenly showed up in the yard, it took us no time to set up an appointment. A flowing and spacious brick split level on a street lined with old ash trees, it had just the space we needed: three roomy bedrooms, a family room, living room, three bathrooms, and an attic office for Richard to work and produce music in. It needed lots of interior work, but in truth we couldn't wait to get at it.

We made an offer, settled on a price in two hours and secured the financing; in no time the keys were ours. A crew of Richard's friends who worked in the construction business showed up the same day we moved in. While the movers were unpacking the truck, the construction crew was busy taking measurements. The day after we moved in, our family room was reduced to studs, an open ceiling and foundation floor.

I'd always loved interior decorating and design, so I took time off from work to settle on the colors, patterns and textures that would help me transition at day's end from my fast-paced job in the manufacturing world to a place where I could bring life to this new space we both called home. I selected neutral, earthy tones and hues, window treatments, linens, dark woods, light fixtures, hardware, appliances and comfy furniture. It would be a comfortable, welcoming space—our forever home—where our children would grow up and our grandchildren would come to visit.

There is a saying that goes like this: if you want to make God laugh, tell him your plans. Two weeks after we moved in, Richard and I had a romantic evening and he had a surprise in store. Getting married was in our immediate plans, but he wanted to make it official and ended the evening by asking me to marry him. It was simple, loving, unrehearsed and even a little awkward. I choked up when he bent down on one knee. I said "YES!" and fell into his arms. We went to sleep that night with our hearts full of the dreams and hopes for our wonderful future ahead.

The next morning, Richard awoke agitated and moody. He felt out of sorts to me. "It feels like the other shoe is going to drop today," he said, "like something is going to go seriously wrong, and I'm scared."

This was completely unlike him, and his words chilled me to my core. But I did my best to reassure him, hugged him extra tight and off we went to work. At the office, I jumped into my usual routine, and before I knew it, it was lunchtime.

Richard called to tell me he was on his way home to work with the construction crew in our family room. His voice was light and happy, and this morning's dark foreboding seemed far away. We both said "I love you" and hung up.

Moments later my world was shattered. I received a phone call telling me that Richard had been involved in a five-car automobile accident. I dropped everything and headed to the hospital, calling the nurses' station on my way. The kind, compassionate nurse told me he was in critical condition, nothing more.

"Critical condition," I repeated to myself. I was positive we would handle this; no matter what injuries he had sustained, we would survive, everything would be OK. When I ran through the trauma-center doors, "they" were waiting—nurses, doctors, Richard's mom—and time stood still. I saw the priest. It was me he was approaching. He grabbed my hands and said, "I'm sorry."

I collapsed. Strangers caught me. Never once, from the moment the call came stating that Richard had been in an accident, did I consider that the outcome might be death. After all, I was 32; he, 33. We were young, with life in front of us. Richard's bright light, energetic smile, limitless creativity, fierce passion—not to mention his love and commitment to me—were gone.

After I got over the shock, the numbness set in. Finally I was able to grasp the reality and started reeling with grief. I asked the question we all ask when a tragedy strikes: Why did this happen to me?

My family had never been very religious. My brother and I were raised Catholic and attended Catholic school, but aside from the occasional wedding or funeral, we did not attend church, so there was no religious doctrine to console me.

I remembered the times Richard and I would talk about life's challenges and I would so often ask that same unanswerable question: Why did this happen to me? And he would say, "Have you no faith Jillbe? God is always here."

But I couldn't find God anywhere in this, and my shattered heart wanted an explanation. I sought out a priest in my new community. If I could just find God, maybe I could understand what happened. But his answer left me feeling hollow. There are, he said calmly, mysteries in life we will never understand.

I located my favorite religion teacher from high school and told her what happened. And in a very calm voice she said, "Do you remember what I taught you Jill? God is everywhere. Begin there."

Richard's words echoed again in my head.

Slowly the comforting words I had learned as a child began to sink back into my head and heart. God was everywhere. I didn't feel as alone or abandoned as I had. Family and friends were a wonderful support in my physical world. But it was the spiritual realm I wanted to know more about.

A friend put me in touch with an incredible psychiatrist who specialized in grief. He gave me the very safest place to fall, one where I could explore to the deepest depths the paralyzing fear for my future. In those early days, I would have slept on his floor if he had let me. I wanted to work my way out of this pain and into this new realm that was before me as quickly as possible. I was intrigued; this unbearable pain was opening new avenues and no matter how hard I tried, I could not rush the process. "Surrender" became a new word in my vocabulary.

And as the saying goes, when the student is ready, the teacher appears.

I continued to work at my job by day and seek peace for my spirit at night. I had nearly taken up residency in the alternative medicine, self-help and psychology sections of local bookstores, where I often took time to sit down and journal about what was happening to me. One day, walking to my favorite bench in the bookstore, a copy of a book titled *Anatomy of the Spirit* by Caroline Myss fell off the shelf and onto the floor in front of me. I didn't know her work but I picked it up and began to read.

The book presents Myss's model of the body's seven centers of spiritual and physical power, in which she synthesizes the ancient wisdom of three spiritual traditions—the Hindu chakras, the Christian sacraments and the Kabbalah's tree of life —to demonstrate the seven stages through which everyone must pass in the search for higher consciousness and spiritual awakening.

Almost overnight, the way I perceived my life changed. I enrolled in classes Caroline taught at her CMED Institute and began to study archetypes from both a psychological and spiritual perspective. I learned about mysticism and the wisdom of saints, how to learn to listen deeply, what a soul's calling is, the difference between fate and destiny and how to discover the incredible treasures of wisdom that lie in the jewel box of my soul. Above all, I learned to trust in something that I couldn't see, yet could energetically sense and feel around me.

These studies directed me to modalities to ease pain and aid in healing. I found CAM (complementary and alternative medicine) and through it was introduced to Reiki, a Japanese technique for stress reduction and relaxation that promotes healing and is based on the idea that an unseen life—force energy flows through us and is what causes us to be alive. Reiki and acupuncture became weekly appointments; they soothed my pain and gave me so much energetic strength that I eventually became a Reiki master (teacher).

Another jewel appeared in my life more than a dozen years ago, when I met one of my dearest friends; to this day she remains my life coach, helping me stay centered, focused and accountable, always striving to become my best self. (I refer to my first session with Glenda as Clarity 101.)

After 20 years in my high-stress role in management, I could feel that my compass was recalibrating, moving me out of that life into a vocation, a life calling. I left my job and happily filled my days studying everything I loved: taking classes in design, reading endless books and mail-order catalogs, spending days at flea markets, antique malls and garage sales, learning the difference between wabi-sabi, vastu shastra and feng shui. Much to my surprise, I already had a combination of all of them under my own roof.

[NOTE: I have always felt very connected to the Japanese concept of wabi-sabi, which represents a comprehensive world-view or aesthetic centered on the acceptance of transience and imperfection. The aesthetic is sometimes described as one of beauty that is "imperfect, impermanent and incomplete." I also admire the principles and precisions of Chinese feng shui, a system of laws considered to govern spatial arrangement and orientation in relation to the flow of energy (qi), and whose favorable or unfavorable effects are taken into account when designing buildings and decorating their interiors. Similarly, vatsu shastra is an ancient science of architecture an construction originating in India that describes principles of design, layout, measurements, ground preparation, space arrangement and spatial geometry. My own experience has been that overall attention is by far more important than following traditional rules to the letter. I invite you to follow your own inner guidance in exploring each of these traditions.]

My life got even busier as I began working with leading authors on spirituality for whom I had the deepest respect. I began traveling the world and delighted in adding other styles and tastes to my design palette: the simplicity and bright colors of India, the stark beauty of the American Southwest, the magical call of nature in South Africa, and the unique charm found in the communities surrounding my native Chicago.

I finally stopped asking why this had happened to me. There are questions that don't need to be answered in life, and that question slowly became a mystery I am at peace with. Why? Because I also see now how the universe supported me through the experience of my loved one's death. As I continually said yes to what I needed for healing and change, another gentle process was at work, and that was the return of my faith—and through this process, I came into gifts I may have never seen otherwise.

Everything I had learned from my experience with Richard's death morphed into something else— a brand new life—and my home had become a reflection of it. As I grieved his loss, I found solace in making my own home into a sanctuary. Without knowing it, for more than a dozen years, I had been training myself for what was next when I thought I was simply coping with my grief. Instead of turning to despair and bitterness, I was guided in a grace-filled direction to a destination I fell in love with. My home became the center of my greatest peace and healing. My need to create a sacred, peaceful environment was my healing path, and I wasn't the only one who liked being there.

People who visit me inevitably mention how peaceful and calm my home is, sinking into the furniture, exhaling and relaxing, breathing in the aroma and scents, feeling the stress melt out of them.

The question I get most often is, "How did you do this?" But my favorite is always, "Can you help me make my home feel like this?"

And the answer to that is a joyful, "Yes I can! That's what this book is about: how you can create your own sacred space.

Let's begin!

CHAPTER ONE

Let's Get Started

Sacred space is where you discover all that is holy in you, around you, and above you. It's where you go to dwell with God.

— Caroline Myss

Welcome!

The goal of this book is to guide you through a process that will help you transform your current living environment into a sacred space — an organized, calm and relaxing reflection of your own individual style that helps create wellness by replenishing your energy and providing inner peace.

You do not have to be wealthy or have a large house to create a space that constantly reminds you of your own deepest values and hopes, and inspires you to realize them. For example, the house I live in now has been furnished on a shoestring. My nightstands come from a hospital in Wyoming and were given to me by a great friend who delivered babies there. The coffee table in my living room is a wooden, hand-whittled chicken coop that is 75 years old. The most expensive feature in my whole house is an Indian poster I received as a gift. Everything else I own was either picked up while traveling, discovered in thrift stores or garage sales — even back alleys on garbage-collection days — and from wonderful, reasonably priced stores like Pier 1. I mention this to make it clear that what you need to create a sacred space is not money, but what each of us already has: creativity, intuitive guidance, imagination and inspiration.

Each chapter will provide you with questions and suggestions designed to help you reflect on both your inner and outer worlds. I recommend that you keep a journal, so you can capture your answers and reflections as you move through the chapters.

The Importance of Home

No matter what place you call home, the very word strikes a chord deep inside each of us. Home means sanctuary, the place we can rest, relax, enjoy time with friends, learn, grow…and just be. Our homes say a lot about who we are and what we think is important in life.

Home is where the heart is but it goes deeper than that. Our connections to home are basic threads in our lives that pop up automatically in casual conversation. We use the word home to identify where we're from (hometown), cheer on players who represent us in sports (home teams), describe a level of comfort (at home), relate to our national identity (homeland), and at the end of a vacation, name it as our favorite next destination ("there's no place like home").

When we commit to a new home, we want it to provide comfort, as well as be a place where we can feel safe and invest our hopes, dreams and wishes as the foundation for our future. Most of us have pretty similar goals and intentions in life, no matter the size, design or geographic location of our homes. We want to start a life with a significant other, perhaps have a family, grow through life's stages and eventually retire. That's the American dream. As our lives progress, the daily demands of family, friends, school, careers—as well as all the unforeseen events we deal with over time—all contribute to the atmosphere in the places we call home.

Think for a moment of your home. If you were to describe it in a word or two, what would it be? Peaceful and calm? Orderly? Disorganized and chaotic? Messy? Open and welcoming? How would you compare the way you describe your home to the life you lead? Our environments are often the exterior reflections of our interior worlds.

Trusting Our Senses—Our Guides to What We Can't See

Think back to the last time you went apartment or house hunting. (Note how we refer to it as a "house" at first. We don't transition to calling it "home" until we begin to think of it as ours) How did you know whether you liked a space when you first walked through the door? Did you smile? Sigh? Check to see where the nearest exit is? What was your first tipoff that the space was a hit or a miss?

Chances are your body told you pretty quickly what your reaction was. We all have a set of intuitive monitors that help us know quickly whether we want to stay in a place or not. They're called our senses. They are an inborn part of our wiring, and with just a little imagination we can call them forth and use them in some pretty creative ways.

These monitors are guiding us twenty-four hours a day, seven days a week. We take them for granted, that we cannot grasp how much we depend on them until we lose them. When a specific sense is limited or removed, we draw upon our memories of what it once provided.

You can test this yourself. Sit at a table and put on a blindfold. Have a friend hand you some items and ask you to identify them by touch alone. Do the same thing with different kinds of food. With the blindfold on, identify some by touch alone, others just by smell, still others by taste. Note how the taste of something is more acute when you cannot see it but have to rely on another sense to identify it.

Each particular missing sense heightens the ones that remain. This is a good exercise for learning to trust our innate ability to navigate our lives by being in touch with the signs our body gives us.

The chapters that follow are designed to provide you with what you will need both inwardly and outwardly to turn your house, apartment, condo or loft into a home of *sacred space*. You will be challenged to use your senses differently and stretch your own ability to "listen" to what they have to tell you.

Each chapter carefully balances the need for awakening both your own inner connection with the Divine and your sacred imagination.

At the end of each chapter, you will find a series of contemplative questions that will help you honestly and richly explore the vision I am inviting you into. These questions will help you become brutally candid with yourself and develop the kind of discipline and courage that you will need to not only turn your home into the most creative and invigorating reflection of yourself, but also provide you with wonder-filled inspiration for your future. I continually follow the same steps I mention here in my own home. Here's what you will need in your toolkit:

- An open mind
- A willing heart
- A journal to keep track of your impressions

About Journaling

You cannot really create the sacred space you need and deserve if you are not paying attention to the shifting circumstances, moods and inspirations of your life. This is why journaling is so important. It not only helps you take note of what you are learning; it also helps you envision a home that truly responds to your deepest inner needs. It is a key component in creating your own sacred space.

Journaling is the art of telling your own story. Its root word, jour, is French for day. So it's a reflection of your day, rather than a story of your life. It's about what you are doing and noticing from day to day— what impressions stick with you. People write journals for many different reasons: to track the ups and downs of new parenthood, to capture the essence of a vacation, to record the impressions of a historical event over time, even to keep track of memorable dreams.

Journaling doesn't require you to be a good writer. (And no one else ever needs to read your journal; it's for your eyes only.) It just requires a little willing discipline—but it's work that pays off. As you write down your responses to the exercises and suggestions in each chapter, you'll discover things you didn't know about yourself. These jewels will help you not only understand the way you see the space you live in but will also help you build—step by step and piece by piece—your own sacred space.

As you journal each day on the questions in each chapter, be honest with your inner self, because that honesty will help you locate your deepest wisdom.

End each entry in your journal with gratitude for what your experiences were on that particular day, good and bad. Our souls grow from these experiences, and so does the sacred environment we are creating.

Writing by hand with paper and pen creates a unique alchemy with your intuitive side, nicely bringing both parts of your brain to bear, but you can also use your computer or tablet. The important thing is to devote regular time to your journaling. If you can journal for an hour, great. If fifteen minutes is all you can handle, fine. What counts most is doing it regularly. You pick the schedule, then stick to it.

Be creative while journaling. Write in different colors using markers, pens or pencils. Add items that call to you, like swatches of paint colors, textures or textiles that inspire you. If you find a beautiful leaf or flower, add it too. Include pictures you have taken that are sacred to you. Think of your journal as your companion in creating sacred space.

I invite you to begin this journey now. Learn how to reinvent *sacred space* in the space of grace that is your home—and the foundation of everything you are and want to be.

Let's get started.

Beginning a Journaling Practice

- Remember: any way you want to journal is fine. Pick what works for you. Use pen or pencil. Add markers or colored pencils. Add drawings, clip art, even small elements from nature to give your journal dimension and grounding. Journaling is a personal experience, so get creative and enjoy it.

- Spend time each day writing and releasing, even if it is only a few lines. Soon you will be pleasantly surprised at what is beginning to take shape.

- Document your dreams; they are messages of guidance from above.

- After a few weeks, go back and revisit what you have written. What patterns do you see? Do you write more or less depending on your mood? Have you noticed any topics that make you feel anxious?

- As you begin to journal, be sure you provide yourself with a comfortable space in your home, or find a quiet spot outside. Be on the lookout for good candidate spaces for yourself.

For many of us, the demands and obligations of life get in the way; work, children, school and daily responsibilities can consume most if not all of our time.

Commit yourself to those 15 minutes to begin and remember this space you're creating is one that creates wellness and replenishes energy and inner peace. As you commit yourself, your sacred space will unfold.

If your writing stalls, try to change your location or surroundings. Are you at your desk? Try a comfy chair or sofa. If you are inside, go outside in the garden or park—even the library is a good change.

Perhaps you need to be inspired by the physical tools of your journaling. Do have a beautiful journal and favorite pen to compose with? If not, what's stopping you from getting them? Indulge yourself! This is your story.

CHAPTER TWO

Sight

For those who look with their physical eyes, God is nowhere to be seen. For those who contemplate Him in spirit, He is everywhere. He is in all, yet beyond all.

—Saint Simeon

The Eyes Have It

A favorite book of mine called The Walk, by William DeBuys, tells the story of a man who walks a lengthy course of his land, time and again over a period of 27 years, in the Southwest. As a reader, I was able to participate and walk alongside him, seeing what he saw.

The author shared the Southwestern landscape in great detail, from the creeks to the woods, and discussed his special relationship with the horses who would just gallop in. As the seasons and years passed, the animals and landscape experienced both subtle and obvious changes. While the story goes on to tell about loss and healing and hardships the author overcame, I was moved moved by the descriptions of what he saw. By focusing on one sense—his sight—he was able to see at an even deeper level with clarity and grace.

After finishing the book, I committed myself to slowing down as often as I could and allowing myself to see what is in my environment by using my peripheral vision—bearing witness to what crossed my path, while trusting what has arrived. As many of us know, we often become so focused on the task that we lose sight of the big picture. How many times have you rushed through the supermarket for those last few items, taking the shortest route, only to stand in a long line waiting impatiently to check out?

When I took the time, I saw the harvest in the produce section—vibrant rich salad tomatoes, round plump pumpkins waiting be carved with jack-o'-lantern faces, many shades of green Granny Smith apples ready to be baked into pies, dented earth-dusted potatoes, bright yellow lemons and ripe bananas all waiting to be picked out thoughtfully and shared with family. In another direction, I found bunches of perfectly opened pink roses or snow-white daisies with their smiley bright-yellow button centers, assorted seasonal pompon carnations and deep-green tropical plants. I would not have seen any of this if I hadn't slowed down. Ironically, when I took the time, the lines were no longer long and my patience was no longer lost.

Each day, my pack of dogs and I take a walk around the neighborhood. Heading out the door of my home is similar to the opening seconds of a horse race when the bell rings, the gate doors open and the announcer says, "And they're off !" Each of the dogs is pulling its weight—and me—down the sidewalk for a relatively short distance, which nonetheless can feel like an eternity. While this initial pulling is happening, I am completely focused on them and what they see, especially their unshakable eagerness in getting to the big cypress tree at the bend ahead. They run and drag me as if it's the first time they've ever seen the tree. Once there, a calm comes over them, their gaits slow, and our walk officially begins.

It's a marvel to watch what all of them see as I participate in their journey. To be headed north and have a leaf tumble east, and immediately all paws head east to catch it—there's nothing like it. We stop at stop signs, waiting to cross as cars pass, and their heads go from right to left in unison, observing the cars in their path. Then there is the occasional ball on a front lawn that all would like to play with, as well as the baby bunnies that appear in the grass near the butterfly bushes at the school playground. It is in these moments that I feel so grateful for my developing sense of seeing more deeply. Had I brought my cell phone or stuffed my iPod headset into my ears, I would have missed the daily routines that fill them with such joyful appreciation and purpose.

Eyes Wide Open — or Closed

It's automatic. When we enter any room, inside or outside, we will locate a focal point, something that draws our eyes to a specific area that, by design, will capture the bulk of our attention. Think of your favorite room right now. What is its focal point? Could it be an architectural feature, such as a fireplace, built-in bookcase, or gorgeous view? Perhaps it is a special picture, mirror, or dramatic piece of furniture. Consider your least favorite room; what is its focal point? Is it the treadmill that has clothing strung all over it that you promise yourself every weekend you will clean up? The torn, dirty sofa in the family room or the stains in the carpet you've never been able to remove?

Focal points usually set a theme that we design a room around. We position furniture in specific ways, we hang artwork in certain locations, and we paint walls particular colors to maximize that focus and draw the eye in that direction. In a kitchen, the focal point can be the island in the center, a corner window or even an appliance. How many times have you rearranged furniture in a room because it just didn't look right? That's the focal point at work.

The focal point allows you to connect with each room of your home and work from the inside out. Your room will feel more balanced, comfortable, and inviting when you arrange the furniture or accessories around a focal point.

Using my home as an example, I have a small 101-year old brown brick ranch with a modest brick fireplace. When you enter my living room from either direction of access, by default you look straight to the fireplace. Only after your eyes land there will you notice the furniture, the art on the wall, the chair in the corner, the coffee table, and the other pieces that occupy space in the room.

Once I established the fireplace as the focal point of my living room, painting walls, arranging furniture and choosing accessories and window dressings became easier. All those decorative items worked in community. Like puzzle pieces, they came together to compliment and accentuate the beauty the fireplace gives the room.

Focal points are everywhere. When we enter a church or temple, we see a crucifix above the altar or a Star of David or a statue of the Buddha. India has the Taj Mahal; New York has the Empire State Building. Chicago has the Sears (now Willis) Tower. Who can miss the dilapidated house in the center of a block of well-groomed homes? The wedding ring on the left hand? The cherry atop the ice-cream sundae? If you look up on a clear dark night, a full moon can be the grandest focal point of all.

We are fortunate to have large living room and kitchen windows in our home. We chose simple blinds as our window coverings. With a twist, we open our inside world and see the most glorious sunrises, sunsets and the moon depending on the time of day. Not to mention the large gingko tree across the street that sways back and forth in the breeze.

Be mindful of windows in each of your rooms. Make sure that they are in good working condition and clean. Consider window treatments that allow Mother Nature in at any time of day.

Journaling about Sight

- How would you describe the interior and exterior of your home?

- Name the focal point(s) in each room.

- What do you like most about your home or apartment?

- What would you most like to change?

Things You Can Do Today

1. Pay attention to how you focus on your surroundings; notice whether you see things while they are moving or active, or still and passive.

2. Be mindful of how you observe the world— whether it is through architecture, nature or color.

3. Do you see with feeling? Has an incredible painting, sculpture, type of architecture every stirred you emotionally? (For example, the works of the Impressionists, Michelangelo's David, the Coliseum in Rome.) Have you stood on the edge of the Grand Canyon and felt its age and the wonder of its existence or watched whales swimming in their pod in the ocean? What does the first fresh snowfall of winter feel like? The first warm day after winter's end?

4. Walk into your favorite room and spend time with it. Close your eyes; when you open them, take note of what you see. Do the same in a room you aren't as fond of and notice the change in your response. Pay attention to whether you wrote more about what was your favorite room or the room you're not fond of.

5. We all have a favorite object in our homes. Name it. Take time to discover something new about it that you haven't noticed before.

6. Notice what you see while in your life routine. Pay attention to whether you see what is new or if you only notice what is missing. Think of the grocery store you drove past for years that suddenly closed, or walking down a once familiar street where buildings have been torn down.

Moving on to the Next Chapter

- What did you learn about your own ability to see and perceive your surroundings?

- How present do you think you are to your world?

Getting ready for work, pause and witness the sunrise. At day's transition into dusk, watch the sunset. Before you go to bed, go outside and look up at the incredible moon. Say a gratitude prayer, because watching the horizon change before your very eyes changes you.

CHAPTER THREE

Smell

Smell is a potent wizard that transports you across thousands of miles and all the years you have lived.

—*Helen Keller*

Psychologists tell us that the sense of smell is the most powerful and evocative sense we have. In an instant, a smell can bring us back to a forgotten moment or experience from our distant past. Scents stir, awaken and enhance our emotional state. Inhaling the perfect selection of scents can bring us to a euphoric place of joy and well-being. Which scents release stress from your body or psyche, bringing you to a place or moment that provides contentment, relaxation or calm? Which exhilarate, motivate or inspire you?

Scents and perfumes radically alter our sense of space. Every person has his or her own favorite scents. I suggest that you make a list of what yours are and note exactly how they make you feel. Consider for a moment these common smells:

- Freshly brewed coffee
- Hot-out-of-the-oven chocolate-chip cookies, apple pie or bread
- Rain
- Just-laundered clothes
- Fresh-cut flowers from the garden
- A sprig of rosemary rubbed between your fingertips
- Incense
- Wood burning in a fireplace on the first cool day of fall
- Freshly cut grass on a summer's day
- Pine needles on a forest floor
- A salty breeze that tells you you're near an ocean

Next time you encounter these pay attention to your breathing as you inhale the scent. Work with your sense of smell consciously and note how you respond. More often than not, when we encounter a smell that touches us emotionally, we inhale deeply in anticipation of what's to come, because at physiological and psychological levels we know what that end feeling will be.

The power of our breath brings us into our core — our chi, energy, or prana. Yoga is a great example of this breath energy at work. Each pose requires coordinated breathing for you to maintain a position and gain its full benefit. The deeper the breath, the easier it is to hold the position, the further our muscles are stretched, and the better the workout.

Even the meditation techniques in all religions are based on breathing. As our breathing gets fuller and deeper, we then relax and open. We feel lighter. As we inhale and exhale, we reconnect to ourselves and all living beings. It cleanses us of toxins, tension and worry.

When introducing new smells to enhance your sacred space, it's best to work with ones that are as natural as possible, because they will have higher vibrations and create energetic shifts within us and in our environment. Lower vibrations are weighed down by artificial fillers. Pure lavender or lemon smell fresher than any artificial lavender or lemon oil mixed with various chemicals.

Natural smells inspire us in a way that manufactured scents never can, and best of all, they don't pollute the atmosphere. Their purity helps align us with our inner source. Essential oils are made from natural substances, carrying the healing energy of their sources. Test essential oils for those that most arouse your senses.

I use Young Living Oils in my sacred space for their spiritually and emotionally uplifting properties. When you use an essential oil, you are holding that pure essence, or scent, of nature. These botanicals can be diffused and inhaled in your home to inspire a positive emotional state, enhance physical wellness, purify your home and create deep spiritual awareness.

Journaling About Smell

- Close your eyes and drift back to your earliest childhood memories. Can you remember the first smell that stuck with you? (Perhaps paste and crayons from school, cough medicine, your mother's perfume or your favorite food cooking on the stove.) Write it down. Then close your eyes and see if you can recall its scent.

- Make a list of your own personal favorite scents and aromas.

- What scents have you noticed in other homes that you would like to have in your own home?

- What smell do you attribute to each room of your house?

- Do you find that when you take in a scent, you close your eyes and inhale deeply and exhale slowly? How do you feel? Are you calm? Excited?

Things You Can Do Today

1. Try identifying your own scent. Women's olfactory senses are far more enhanced during menstruation and pregnancy. And both women and men's scents increase after exercise, sex or dancing. If you'd like to alter your own scent, consider musk to accentuate it or patchouli or sandalwood to balance it. Consider fresh florals such as jasmine or rose to uplift and inspire.

2. Identify your home's scent (if you don't know, ask a friend to describe what they smell when they walk in your door).

3. Use fresh herbs when you cook and savor the fresh smells.

4. Introduce new scents into your home.

5. Bring seasonal flowers from the garden or market inside. (Do this throughout the year.)

6. Spritz your favorite scent on your curtains or throw pillows.

Moving on to the Next Chapter

- How will you incorporate your sense of smell into your sacred space?
- Has anything you learned surprised you?

Because it's best to use natural fragrances and products throughout your home, spend a little time finding a good local or online provider. Add both incense and essential oils to your sacred space. In my experience, ylang-ylang* makes people joyful. Most spiritual bookstores carry a range of incenses and oils.

*Pronounced E-lon(g) E-lon(g)

CHAPTER FOUR

Sound

Hear one side and you will be in the dark. Hear both and all will be clear.

— *Lord Chesterfield*

The power of sound to alter both our mood and the ways in which the colors and textures dance in our sacred space is one of the great hidden secrets you need to know to lift living in your sacred space to new levels of power and inspiration.

I live on a quiet tree-lined street in a Chicago suburb, a short block off a main road. I rarely hear sirens or the hustle and bustle common to many busy urban communities, with the exception of an occasional passing truck or speeding car— or the sound of my neighbor, who announces himself with the rev of his Harley on his way down the block. Since I live in quiet surroundings, these occasional loud noises still startle me no matter how many times I hear them.

In the evening, I frequently hear the overnight freight trains in the distance, on their way into Chicago. There is a dull hum to the rickety wheels scraping along the iron tracks. Lying in bed, it is often this consistent sound of the train cars at maximum speed that actually lulls me to sleep. When I am out of town, I miss the sound of those train cars, because it's a familiar sound in my life.

Whether you live in a noisy neighborhood or a peaceful and quiet one, you adjust to the presence or absence of noise, and that becomes your "normal." Interestingly, both ways of living might rely on white noise, either to help drown out external noises or complement the silence (personally, I love the sound of my electric fan).

Have you noticed that we as a society have become almost immune to certain noises? Many times I have been stuck in city traffic when an ambulance or police car has come rushing up beside me, sirens blaring, on its way to an emergency. Around me I can see other drivers paying no attention, talking or texting on their phones or zoning out with earbuds plugged in, their heads bobbing in time to music, blocking out the outside noise with inside noise. We have all gotten very good at shutting down and turning off.

Once I was privileged to make a pilgrimage to the Chartres Cathedral in France, where I had the pleasure of experiencing that sacred space amplified by the sound of a gifted cellist who played without written music, simply closing his eyes and being present to whatever notes and tempo he received as divine inspiration. Each person in the audience instinctively knew to remain in reverent silence to help enable his wonderful performance.

As his bow moved expertly across the cello strings, the massive vaulted ceilings in this breathtaking medieval stone cathedral carried every note perfectly, distributing the sound evenly throughout. We could literally feel the notes in our bodies. As the music touched something deep within our souls, as our hearts opened wide to the experience. Many in the group wept.

Silence — The Absence of Sound

At one time or another, each of us has been called to spend time in silence. For some it is a major adjustment because of one simple truth: we have had no experience with the absence of sound or the great stillness within that accompanies it. True silence is so complete that you can hear your own heart beat. To be in silence is to be called into your soul. Discovering it is a great gift.

Everything that is alive has its own sacred sound, much different from created, manufactured ones. Some of them may not be audible. Bring your awareness to all living things when you are moving about your day. Begin to consciously listen to the sounds—or silence—that are an innate part of nature: wind, rain and trees. Tune in to the silent work of snowflakes falling on a cold winter evening. Turn off the outside lights, wrap yourself in warmth and go outside. Then just listen to this great magical stillness. Note how snow acts as soundproofing and quiets everything. Enjoy the way you are touched inside on a deeper level. This is nature teaching you the healing power of stillness.

The Sounds of Your Life

Make a list of your favorite sounds and your favorite kinds of music—and of the kinds of moods, emotions and perceptions each one stirs in you. Become a secret alchemist of your own moods by using the sounds and music you like to lift you constantly into your richest and most joyful self.

When I am feeling down, I love to put on Tina Turner. When I feel a need to connect with my inmost self, I listen to Gregorian chants or the luminous works of Bach. Sometimes as I work in Chicago, I long for natural sounds and love to fill my room with the melody of ocean waves or simple birdsong. Throughout my day, I check in and ask myself, "What would I like to feel now?" or "What emotion do I want to invite in at this moment?" And

I choose the music accordingly—because that's what music can do for us.

When I have people over and want the atmosphere in my whole house to be full of joy and welcome, I'll put on jazz and soft R&B. When I light the candles before my guests come in, the whole house seems to be dancing with me.

Some sounds serve multiple purposes; for example, the glorious ringing of bells, tingshas (two small cymbals attached to a cord), drums, finger cymbals, crystal drums, gongs, wind chimes or Tibetan music bowls all help us connect with the Divine directly.

Journaling about Sound

- Is there any type of music you resist? Why? Under what circumstances would you be willing to be open to it?

- Write about the times when sounds have helped you work through either a tough or joyous occasion (for instance a wedding or funeral).

- Explore whether you are moved by percussion, strings or vocals and why.

- If you play a musical instrument, enjoy how it sounds in your sacred space and how it resonates in the core of your body. How do your space and your body interact in this moment?

* Pay attention to the noise inside (TVs, heaters or air conditioning) and outside (traffic, lawn equipment, emergency vehicles) your home and note how it affects your mood.

* What everyday sounds would you miss if you could no longer hear them?

Things You Can Do Today

1. Play your favorite music each day and dance like it is the first time you've heard it—really dance. Let your body respond and express itself with the sounds that surround you. Get your mojo back!

2. Commit to listening to music you might not normally listen to. You may actually discover something new.

3. Learn to chant.

4. Open a window and introduce nature sounds into your home (second choice: a sound machine—even most smart phones today offer apps that do this).

5. Add meditation music as a calming background in your home.

6. Spend a complete day in silence—note all you hear.

Moving on to the Next Chapter

* How will you find more time to connect with the sacred power of music (other than singing in the shower)?

* How will connecting with music enhance your sacred space?

Everything that is alive has its own sacred sound, much different from the created, manufactured ones. Some of them may not be audible. As you move about your day, make a point of being more conscious of the sounds in your life. Listen to the wind, rain and trees, or the stillness and quiet of a snowflake falling on a cold winter's eve—you will be touched inside on a deeper level. Express yourself even further with a form of sacred or cosmic dance. Let your body respond to the sounds that surround you.

CHAPTER FIVE

Touch

Touch comes before sight, before speech. It is the first language and the last, and it always tells the truth.

—Margaret Atwood

When you walk into any room in your home, what do you want to touch? What moves you to reach out and make that physical connection?

Touch is the only sense that involves the whole body. In the human embryo it is the first sense to develop; after birth, it is a baby's primary tool for learning about its environment. Touch connects us with life. In our homes, touch speaks to our need for comfort and beauty. When creating your own sacred space, it helps to know what draws both your eye and hand. What appeals to you and what combinations just feel right to you?

The feel and gleam of the surfaces and fabrics you use in your sacred space are an important complement to the colors you choose. Take time to decide how you want those colors and textures to work together. Ask yourself what mood you want to establish in each room.

Making the interior of your home into a space that invites a second look is a skill. The materials that surround us in our homes have an enormous impact on us. Different textures bring richness to design when opposites like rough and smooth, crumpled and glossy, dull and glittering, and soft and hard coexist in close proximity. The more you enjoy playing with such opposites, the more exciting and provocative your sacred space will become.

The Beauty of Textiles

The textiles in our homes come in many forms and textures, from carpets and rugs to quilts and linens, from wall hangings and window treatments to throws and furniture upholstery. Whether woven or knitted, natural or synthetic, fiber or cloth, textiles add luster to our homes and excite our sense of touch.

Become fully acquainted with what ignites your sense of touch. Is it thick velvet draperies? Crisp cotton or delicate lace curtains? Maybe it's a puffy white down blanket or a deep, worn leather sofa or soft suede oversized chair. Are you bedazzled by luxurious silk or satin pillow coverings? When you are truly inspired by your textile choices, your rooms will radiate your innate personality.

Take a look at the textiles in each room and decide whether they fill a functional need or simply appeal to your senses (or both). We use textiles to add color, draw attention to focal points or create and maintain an ongoing theme with repeated patterns or colors.

Texture Patterns

Make a careful inventory of the texture patterns in each room and how they make each room unique. Perhaps you will list rich hardwood floors, accent woods (think reclaimed barn wood or old wooden beams) or exposed brick walls, or maybe deep plush carpet, smooth or tumbled stone or tile floors? Metal handrails or hardware on cabinets? Granite countertops? Stainless-steel appliances? What do your lighting fixtures look like? Do you have grand chandeliers? How about soft, illuminating sconces? Mix and match different styles you like to create your own. That is the beauty of sacred space, it is the reflection of you, your soul. There is no wrong way to do it.

As you create your sacred space, be mindful of the materials and textures that you don't care for. Most of us can think of a piece or two in each room (either furniture or accessories) that we could live without; yet for some reason, we don't remove them.

Be creative. Slipcovers are an easy, reasonable solution (often, so is reupholstering). Trading, donating, recycling and going to garage sales are other options. If you want to change floors, cabinetry or fixtures, do-it-yourself kits are easy to find and let you recoat, stain or paint what you have to live with until you can replace it.

As you begin to sort out what you love from what you don't, be sure that what you consciously fill your home with consists of furniture, accessories, window treatments, flooring, appliances, clothing, hardware, linens, wall treatments and lighting pieces that speak to you and bring balance to your room.

What's Your Style?

The style and textures we choose for our homes are external reflections of our interior selves. Here is a brief description of some common styles found in homes today. Use it to help you define your signature style.

Country

Country rooms exude warmth and coziness. Elements such as pottery and baskets have a handmade, rustic quality. Stone, tile and brick are common features. Wooden surfaces and coarse materials are reflected in furnishings, accessories, floors and walls. Natural colors give the room a rich and earthy feel. Checked, floral and striped vintage fabrics are standards.

Traditional

Rooms with a traditional style are calm, elegant and organized. Subtle textures can help create a more relaxed and casual feel. The color palette usually includes neutral tones such as beige, light gray and light pink, and fabrics are muted—usually simple florals, solids, plaids or stripes. Accessories are arranged in matched sets and predictable patterns.

Contemporary

Contemporary design often has clean, sleek lines and is usually marked by predominantly muted neutrals or bold solid colors. Space is a key element when arranging furniture. Each piece should be noticed on its own while adding harmony to the room. Furniture is sleek, lower to the ground and frequently has metal frames or straight legs with emphasis on basic shapes and forms.

Eclectic

This style is always in motion, because it invites newness and evokes a sense of imagination. When done right, it's both unpredictable and fun. An eclectic style borrows from several other design styles to create a unique look. Working with this style can be tricky, because it requires skill to keep elements from clashing or being so different that a room looks and feels chaotic. A multitude of fabrics is characteristic—textured, solids, patterned or all three.

Mixing and Matching

Don't feel confined to just one style—draw inspiration from wherever you find it and weave together your own sacred space. In our home, I have paired Indian silk pillows with more rugged South African fabrics. Atop weather-worn barn furniture I have mixed a hand-carved giraffe and elephant from the bushveld of South Africa with a radiant golden Shiva statue from Chindambaram in South India.

When I see and feel these accessories I am immediately transported back to these amazing journeys abroad, ever grateful for the memories and able to visit them again and again.

What Our Closets Say about Us

Take a close look at your closets and drawers. They reflect with uncanny precision your inner life.

Our clothes selections dress our moods and emotions. They enhance or protect our personas in the world daily.

Pay attention to how you organize these items. For instance, a Type A personality such as myself may have all their clothes in color order, short sleeve to long sleeve and from lightest to darkest. All clothing likely faces the same way on identical hangers. Same goes for shoes: dress shoes on one side, casual on the other.

While I don't want to impose my own Type A personality, I can't help thinking organizing in this way would vastly help order lives. Clothes organizing businesses make millions of dollars for this specific reason.

Expanding Touch

There are many other elements of touch to consider outside of textiles. Consider the shape and texture of sculptures you might have: the smoothness of a marble tray, the ruggedness of a wood carving. Consider the accessories in your rooms such as books, vases and candles. Consider the tile or hardwood on your floors, materials you choose for carpets or throw rugs—are they shaggy and plush, or rough like jute?

What materials are your plates and glasses made of? Think of the handles of your silverware and knives. All are created with your sense of touch in mind.

Go outside in your front yard or backyard and feel the earth and grass beneath your bare feet. Do you meld into the earth and exhale a sense of calm? If you have concrete, bricks or stone as walkways, how do they stimulate your sense of touch?

Journaling about Touch

- What style predominates in your home's interior? Is it the same as when you moved in or have you changed it? If you kept or changed it, can you say why you did?

- What is the mood/intention of each of your rooms? What textures help create it?

- Take a look again at the contents of your closet. What comparisons can you make between your clothing and your personal choices?

- What is your favorite piece in each room? Can you think of textures that would enhance its beauty?

Things You Can Do Right Now

1. For a quick, instant change in a room, interchange pillows, linens or throws among the rooms in your home.

2. Buy yourself a luxurious article of clothing and note how you feel in it.

3. Pay special attention to textures you see and how you are stimulated by them.

4. Sleep on 400-count pure cotton sheets (or better yet, 800) and note how much better they feel than synthetics or blends. It does your body good!

5. After a shower or bath, dry your body with a thick absorbent cotton towel.

Moving on to the Next Chapter

- How are you becoming more aware of textures that excite you now?

- What changes can you make to illuminate these textures in your rooms and bring out their qualities even more?

Go exploring and fine-tune your own sense of style.

- Visit a large home-furnishings store or one of the do-it-yourself superstores and explore the range of textures and surfaces available. Touch them whenever possible!

- Haunt local garage sales, flea markets, thrift shops, consignment shops, antique markets— even back alleys—for treasures you can reclaim with your own creative flair. (So much more fun than always buying from a chain.)

- Not completely sure of what your style is? Tear out pages from magazines, books, newspapers or furniture advertisements for ideas on room styles, décor or design ideas you like. Keep them in a file. In no time you will see a pattern of materials and textures begin to emerge.

PART 2

You in Your Space

Home is a place we all must find, child. It's not just a place where you eat or sleep. Home is knowing. Knowing your mind, knowing your heart, knowing your courage. If we know ourselves, we're always home, anywhere.

—Glinda, the Good Witch of the North, from the film The Wizard of Oz

JILL ANGELO

CHAPTER SIX

Self-care

The body, being the temple of the living spirit, should be carefully tended in order to make it a perfect instrument.

—*Swami Vishnudevananda*

Creating a style that is uniquely you doesn't start with list making and trips to the paint store. At the end of the day, every room in your home is a reflection of your interior world. In other words, what you wish to create externally can only reflect what you practice internally. That's why creating your own sacred space requires you to take a fearless inventory of your own body and how you care for it.

Our bodies are temples, but more often than not we treat them like machines. We expect them to deliver, to run on empty, to never give in, to never break down and to always go that extra mile. Eventually, however, something will cause us to slow down—or even come to a complete stop—forcing us to look more closely at the way we are treating ourselves.

For instance, consider the person who has a regular exercise routine that she doesn't veer from.

She works out regularly and can feel her endorphins kicking in, helping her function at a clearer, higher energetic level. She drinks the recommended eight glasses of water every day, takes vitamins, eats healthy food and avoids skipping meals. She is confident, focused and tuned in to the messages her body sends her. When you put good into your body (good nutrition, good habits, good responses to bodily signals), you reap good as well. On a spiritual level, your interior world reflects who you are to yourself in deep privacy—your dreams, your desires, your hopes. Your exterior world is your world of social obligation, career and economic range.

Contrast this with someone who has been told to lose weight, exercise more and make wiser food choices but chooses to go instead for the quick fix, buying exercise equipment, joining weight-loss programs and loading up on supplements without ever committing to any action. In this case, the person is acting as a result of outside pressure and not internal motivation—the exterior is indeed a reflection of the interior world.

Contrast this with someone who has been told to lose weight, exercise more and make wiser food choices but chooses to go instead for the quick fix, buying exercise equipment, joining weight-loss programs and loading up on supplements without ever committing to any action. Intention without action is a hallmark of the exterior world not matching the interior world.

Ask yourself this. In which of these people's homes would you expect to find order and calm? Chaos and tension? When you truly honor your body as a temple, you become more conscious about how you live. You also become accountable to yourself for the way you feel. Your outer behavior becomes an extension of your inner world.

Taking the First Step

Most of us get very good at putting our own needs last, after the demands of families and careers. We work more and sleep less. Exhaustion sets in, and it can get very hard to keep our promises to ourselves.

The good news is that it's easy to get started. Here are three simple ways to honor body, mind and spirit.

Body

Do you really know what's in the food you eat? Investigate the food that's in your pantry and refrigerator. Feed yourself healthy nourishing foods for energy and hydration. Avoid GMOs (genetically modified organisms) by learning to read food labels, and stay away from processed food as much as possible (especially fast-food drive-up windows).

Mind

A great way to honor and cherish your body is to meditate a little every day to help reduce stress, anger and anxiety, to clear the chattering "monkey" mind that drives us all. When you sit calmly and quietly, focus on your breathing and let your thoughts pass through you rather than consume you, it has a healing effect; try it for 10 minutes in the morning and before you go to sleep each night. You'll find that you have more energy, gratitude and joy throughout the day.

Spirit

Take a walk. Listen to the sounds around you. Sit in a park and see how many shades of green you can pick out. Feel how your body and mind respond. When you've sat there long enough to sigh, that's your interior world thanking you for letting it reconnect to the source of life.

Journaling about Self-care

- On a scale of one to 10 (with 10 being your ideal), what number best suggests your commitment to your sacred space within — your commitment to self-care?

- What is your fuel? What is hiding in your pantry/fridge that needs to go? Are you set up for healthy eating?

- What better choices might you make in your daily routine to help create a healthier regimen of self-care?

- How do you neglect yourself by putting yourself last?

- What practices do you currently have in place that give you energy? How can you maintain or extend these practices?

Things You Can Do Today

1. Stay away from fast-food drive-through windows and note how much better you feel.

2. Begin a simple exercise program. Walking is excellent!

3. Take vitamins every day.

4. If you can afford a nutritionist, visit a holistic one; if not, Google holistic nutrition and investigate on your own.

5. Meditate or just sit outside where it's quiet for ten minutes.

6. Laugh.

7. Make realistic "to do" lists (we seldom honor the unrealistic ones).

8. Get a massage.

9. Celebrate mealtime. Use the good china and silver, and drink from the crystal goblets.

Moving on to the Next Chapter

- Decide to become more involved in taking care of yourself than you ever have before. Tell friends about it so they can support your lifestyle change.

- Create a daily exercise and nutrition plan as a discipline to keep you on track.

Many people in India begin their day at sunrise, cleansing themselves in the Ganges River and offering up the water in gratitude to the divine for their life and blessings. As you take your shower or settle into your bath, invoke the same intention and reverence. Give thanks for your life. As you cleanse your body, release the stress, anxiety, fear and worry. Let it run down the drain with the water.

CHAPTER SEVEN

Color

Life is like a train of moods, like a string of beads, and as we pass through them they prove to be colored lenses.

—*Ralph Waldo Emerson*

The vibration of color is the essential foundation for our created environment. Color surrounds us: our clothes, cars, jewelry, offices and most important, our homes. The colors we choose express our deepest personalities and are the external representations of our souls.

The amazing gift of color is the almost instantaneous way it can transform our homes, a room or object and, consequently, us.

Many great painters have written passionately about the emotional and spiritual qualities associated with color. To create your own sacred space, you will need to take a journey with how color makes you feel.

When I am in South Africa, my palette of color selections are matte camouflage greens and sandy desert browns. When in India, a place where everything seems to have a gold thread glimmering through it, I am intoxicated by turquoise, orange and red.

Imagine now a room in pure white that represents your inner purity and calm. While being in the peaceful state that this pure white engenders, notice how your body responds by exhaling and relaxing. If you were to cover that same room with a coat of deep red paint, your body would likely respond with excitement and a faster heartbeat. What happens when you visualize the color yellow instead? Does it make you smile and think of the sun? In so many ways, color can radically shift the depth and vibration of a room without your having to change anything else.

You may remember from grade school that each color emits different frequencies of light or energies that we could call vibrations. In so many ways, color can radically shift the depth and vibration of a room without your having to change anything else.

Color also has a direct effect on your moods. It can lift or deflate your spirits. Think of going outside and looking up into a cloudless summer sky of brilliant blue. How will this gorgeous sun-filled day affect you? Now consider that same sky as a storm moves in and turns an ashen gray with muted greens against the blackening clouds rolling in. Next time you have a chance to experience that transition from color and light to dark, note how your body reacts and how your mood shifts.

Color on a Universal Level

Color has a tremendous influence in shifting the way we feel, and it's a gateway to understanding ourselves more deeply. In the great mystical systems, color has an ancient and sacred role. Red in Hinduism signifies life energy and the divine feminine. Green in Sufism represents the eternally fresh truth of the heart. Gold in Buddhism represents the world as seen through enlightened eyes. Purple in many traditions is the color for divine love and unconditional compassion. In many cultures white exemplifies the white divine light that creates everything, while in Asian traditions it characterizes death. Blue is the sacred color for the Mother (Mary) and in Christianity.

Here is a general list of colors and their meanings:

* Black: strength, independence, power, and mystery
* Brown: grounding, stability, genuineness
* Blue: patience, calm, faith, trust
* Green: harmony, health, growth, balance, wealth

- Orange: vitality, abundance, warmth, excitement
- Pink: love, compassion, kindness
- Purple: inspiration, intuition, wisdom, imagination
- Red: courage, passion, stimulation, emotion
- Yellow: cheerfulness, confidence, happiness, joy
- White: purity, simplicity, clarity, peace, cleanliness, calm

When exploring color in your home, select one room at a time. If you need some color choices for inspiration, consult the color wheels at your local paint or home design store. They offer a staggering array of possibilities and break down the selections by hue (color), tint (color plus white), tone (color plus gray), and shade (color plus black) for easy matching. Then give each room your focused attention. Try sitting quietly with your eyes closed and let the room's essence sink into your consciousness. Be patient. The walls will "talk" to you.

Another way to begin selecting colors is to take a good long look at your closet and drawers. This will acquaint you again with your favorite colors. In your creation of sacred space, take some risks with color and extend your normal choices to embrace colors that could take you to a new place in your life. When I first moved into my house, each room and ceiling had been painted a simple beige, so I had a clean palette to start with.

That simple beige was like a flat line, neutral, blah and boring. Instead, I wanted the rooms to burst alive with color and the vibrations. The first thing I did was to get a paint chart and have at the rooms. I chose colors named "Chocolate Covered Cherries" and "Desert Canyon" for my living room, "Chivalry Copper" and "Parakeet Green" for my kitchen, "Chocolate" and "Rain" for my office. The house came alive room by room, each with a different vibration or pulse to it. Then I chose textures to match, then accessories, and before I knew it, the house was as passionate and alive as me.

Ask yourself if you feel ready for a more vibrant color scheme. I find that when I am ready to take greater risks in my life, I am also ready to risk bolder colors in my home.

In India, people add crushed crystals, holy water, ash or essential oils to the paint they use to cover their walls. They do this to infuse the whole home with sacred blessing. I highly recommend this practice.

While in the process of selecting colors, consider the overall intention of the room you are choosing the specific color for. Before painting, sit with the color in the room it was selected for, reflecting on this intention. If you want to add sacred components, this is the time to do so. Remain mindful of your intention when adding a few drops of your favorite essential oil, holy water or ash, and stir well. To add crystals, crush a small piece of crystal in a plastic bag with a hammer until it becomes a powder. I wouldn't add more than a teaspoon. Stir well into the paint can.

Journaling on Color

- What was your favorite color when you were a child? What is your favorite color now? Where do you find yourself most often using that color?

- How do you now see yourself through the colors you choose?

- What patterns and colors did you find when you inventoried your closet and drawers?

- If you had to choose one color to live with, what would it be? (Note: it isn't always your favorite color.)

Things You Can Do Now

1. Repaint a room you don't care for and note the instant change in the way it feels to you.

2. Now assess what's in each room again, this time considering the list of color meanings. Knowing a color's mystical meaning adds another dimension to your awareness of how you put a room together. (See how intuitive you are?)

3. Wear a different color to work each day. Be aware of how it affects your day, especially your productivity.

4. Introduce your favorite colored flowers throughout your home and notice how it instantly changes the way the room feels to you.

Moving on to the Next Chapter

* Color surrounds all aspects of our lives. How will you introduce new colors into your daily life?

* If you had to choose one color to live with, what would it be? (Note: it isn't always your favorite color.) It works best to introduce new decorative items in odd-numbered lots. So

consider one big new vase, three new pillows or—depending on size—five, seven or nine frames, candles or flowers for your room.

- Introduce a dash of a new color into a room by using linens, throw pillows or flowers. Notice the change in your visual and emotional perceptions as a result. Each room will undergo a shift in energy. Can you feel it?

It works best to introduce new decorative items in odd-numbered lots. So consider one big new vase, three new pillows or—depending on size—five, seven or nine frames, candles or flowers for your room.

CHAPTER EIGHT

Nature

In all things of nature there is something of the marvelous.

—Aristotle

Nature in its beauty, wildness and magnificence is God's greatest gift to us and constantly invites us into a deeper gratitude for, and unity with, every living being. It is a sacred component of our outer and inner lives—and of our homes. Nature calms, inspires, refreshes and purifies the energy of a home or office. Bringing it inside with us enhances creative thought and balances our bodies, minds and souls. The more we appreciate nature and incorporate it into our living spaces, the calmer and more our spaces harmonize a calmer psychological and spiritual atmosphere.

Look around your home. Every item in it comes from nature, whether in its original form or crafted from other natural materials: towels and sheets from cotton, plates from glass (which in turn comes from sand and stone), rugs and upholstery from fiber, tables and chairs from wood. In every room, you can see where nature surrounds you—from the glass in your windows to the bricks in your fireplace, from tile or bamboo floors to walls made of wood planking, plaster or drywall (a creative combination of sand, water and gypsum). Even our metal fixtures and appliances come from elements mined from the earth. Nature is everywhere in our lives, both inside and out; it's the essence of creativity.

Mother Nature's Heavenly Palette

Always welcome the experience of nature in your everyday life. When you make your color choices, select the muted colors of the earth and trees, the calm blues of the waters, the vibrancy of the brightly colored flowers that are your favorites.

Look to the seasons and the Mother Nature's life cycles, which provide extraordinary palettes of landscape and climate. We cycle through these passages time and again, but each change has its own particular joy and exquisite way of anticipating the new. Welcome these changes and stages with plants and flowers, fruits and vegetables. Always choose organic varieties because the energy, Mother Nature's blessing to us, is more pure.

Let There Be Light

If your window treatments are shutting out natural light with blinds or draperies, consider opening

Lucia's Garden

2360 West Alabama   Houston, TX 77098
713/523-6494

NAME	Anglica Altinger - green					
ADDRESS						

		PH. NO.		DATE 4·21·16		
SOLD BY	CASH	C.O.D.	CHARGE	ON ACCT.	MDSE. RETD.	LAYAWAY
			CASH			

QTY.	DESCRIPTION	PRICE	AMOUNT	
	Votive		4	95
(B)	Sacred Space		14	99
			19.	94
			1	65
			21.	59
		TAX		
RECEIVED BY		TOTAL		

No. 173524

ALL CLAIMS AND RETURNED GOODS
MUST BE ACCOMPANIED BY THIS BILL.

GP-154-2
PRINTED IN U.S.A.

Thank You

them up to welcome the divine sunrises, sunshine, clouds and sunsets into your sacred space. While there are many lighting options available, pure, clean, natural light from the source is best for our overall health and well-being.

Leave as many windows open for fresh air and light as you can. Our homes become stagnant and dull without fresh air circulating throughout to cleanse the accumulating toxins brought on by daily life. We all know how great our homes feel and smell after a good dose of spring cleaning (whatever the season). Cleaning is a powerful practice because it washes out staleness and darkness. By opening our doors and windows, we keep pure energy flowing in, moving psychic weight out.

Living Cooperatively in Our Environment

The more we surround ourselves with nature by using natural things (and not artificial or inferior materials like compressed sawdust, which can be full of formaldehyde resins), the better it is for our bodies and souls. By furnishing our homes with natural elements, we help find the natural balance that keeps the outside at bay but nature as close as the cloth we wear and sleep in.

Develop your green thumb by planting trees, flowers and a vegetable or herb garden. Use recycled materials rather than buying new ones, and don't forget the greatest recycled material of all: compost. Composting is easy and it helps put you into the feedback cycle of life. It's important to be mindful of what you take from the earth and to make a conscious commitment to give back. When you are finished harvesting from your garden, don't throw the old plants and dead stalks in the trash. Instead, roll them back into the earth by adding them to your compost pile.

Have plenty of plants and flowers indoors (the additional oxygen is good for you). Not much space? Plant a window herb garden or flower box in a bright, sunny spot. Take a minute every day to enjoy its colors and aromas. Pay attention to your overall mood after you do. This helps you experience the joy of nature and its effects in new ways. (And don't forget to add them to your compost pile when they're done showing off for you.)

Flowers let us get closer to nature by bringing the outdoors in, and this also has a rich and positive effect on our moods. The arrangements enhance the colors of each room with elegance, whether it is a single artfully placed flower or a full arrangement bristling with color and life.

Nature as a Memory in Your Space

Nature also exists in our memories. Think of an amazing place you have traveled to. What part of nature spoke to your soul and created a sense of homecoming? Sometimes the places we visit need time to settle before we realize their profound effect on us. We may long for what we remember of a trip and try to duplicate the experience at home by cooking the food or drinking the wine that lets us revisit the experience. Have those memories made their way into your home?

Of all my travels, South Africa calls me home time and again with her irresistible voice. My soul is nurtured by the vastness of the land, the lack of light and noise pollution, the constellations illuminating the southern night sky, the brownish-yellow thatched grass and deep red clay-colored sand with its embedded shimmering crystals. It happens so effortlessly. When I visit there, I live in a circular mud and clay rondavel (hut) and am awakened early in the morning by the roar of lions and leopards and the call of the many bush babies of the bushveld. Being submerged in nature like this both rejuvenates and calms me. It's an incredibly different life from the one I lead back in Chicago.

Most of what I bring back from South Africa is very simple and inexpensive: I have many coffee-table books that hold the incredible images of that native land, baobab trees, bush animals, local communities, rondavels and statues. I love to shop, literally on the side of the road, for the wooden bowls, giraffes and elephants whittled by locals, along with deep earth-toned textiles—placemats, towels or woven tapestries that can be hung on the wall or strung across the bed for an instant earthy, grounding appeal. Lastly I have many shimmering, solid, flat stones filled with ancient heritage that I find while walking that magnificent land.

A Native American shaman once called me a "stone person" because of my love for stones. Collecting them from all over has become a tradition of mine. I can be out walking and suddenly a stone will grab my attention. When I pick it up and hold it in my hand, I can feel its energy connect with mine. A sense of peace and calm comes over me. Having them distributed throughout my home keeps a central grounded energetic force that always seems to calm me, even on the most chaotic day. This shaman taught me that when Mother Earth consents to my taking away a piece of her beauty, I must always give back with an offering. He gave me a small pouch that held sacred tobacco, which I carry with me when I travel.

I have brought back many things from my travels that help me remember the wonders of the places I have visited and the good memories I carry with me. And so can you. When you display the artifacts, textiles, trinkets and other art you have collected on your travels throughout your home, it sets up a template that in one glance can transport you back to the wonderful time and space of that visit. This deeply personal touch not only gives your sacred space character and definition, it also keeps your connection to that place alive in your heart.

Pets — The Nature We Live With

Pets are magnificent gifts to our lives. They are incredible beings that model unconditional love and teach us our own capacity for compassion. The rewards we receive from them are limitless. As I write this, I am surrounded by several mixed breed rescue dogs and one rescued cat. Every day I am greeted again and again by four wagging tails, and our mutual joy fills my soul with gratitude.

Spend time each day with your animals and be in their presence. Watch, feel and listen to the messages they give you. When they bark, whistle, sing, meow, whinny, or neigh, watch their body language and try to decipher what they are communicating. As they so lovingly come to you with a toy (playtime!), make the time; give into the joy that is their gift to you. Share in their love and receive it. Their love is such a powerful, unconditional blessing. Remember that we don't just choose them, they choose us and when they do, it is a lifetime commitment.

Animal rights is my passion and sacred space in my home is also a sanctuary for my dogs, cat and fostered dogs from various shelters. One of the things that makes me happiest is to see all of my animals lying together as a pack.

If you can't rescue animals or have pets where you live, you can still do great good. Every animal organization would love your help. The Internet can direct you to a cause that will fit you.

Note: Please see Chapter 9, Altars, for other ways to incorporate nature into your sacred space.

Journaling on Nature

- What season(s) are you drawn to and why?

- What is your favorite animal? What animal spirits call to you? How do you identify with them?

- Are any of the color selections made in your home inspired by nature? If so, stand in that room and then go into one that isn't. What changes do you note?

Things You Can Do Today

1. Plant a garden. If you can't, create a window herb garden, join in with a community garden, or go to your local farmer's market regularly.

2. Be sure to have plants in your office. They are an absolute life force. They help elevate the oxygen levels and brighten up monochromatic workspaces. If you have a home office, add fresh flowers occasionally or keep a plant nearby.

3. Put a birdbath or feeder in your yard for our feathered friends.

4. Swap out your silk flowers or plants for fresh real ones and feel the difference in the energy in the room.

5. Switch to using as many green products as you can throughout your home.

6. Recycle, compost and cut back on your carbon footprint.

Moving on to the Next Chapter

- How will you implement being more "green" inside—and outside—your home?

- How do you welcome seasonal changes into your sacred space?

Even without a green thumb, herbs are easy to grow indoors year around and not only provide lovely aromas but allow you to add a whole palette of flavor to food.

CHAPTER NINE

Altars

You can't always retreat from the world to a country house, the seashore or the mountains, but it is always in your power to retreat into yourself.

—Marcus Aurelius

Knowing how to create altars is a beautiful and inspiring way to heighten your home's sacred atmosphere and help you to align simply and seamlessly with the Divine.

There is no certain size, shape or specific location for an altar (indoors or out), but before you select a place, take some time to focus and be guided by your own spirit to the best area. To furnish your altar, bring flowers you especially love, icons of deities or sacred teachers you feel especially close to, and add found objects, family photos, candles, crystals, prayer beads, or affirmations written on small pieces of paper as prayers. Arrange the objects you have selected into relationships that speak vibrantly to you. If you like, place them on your favorite cloth. To keep the sacred energy of your altar alive, consider using fire (a candle or the occasional stick of incense) or blessed holy water.

Notice that as you walk through your home, there are many structures and surfaces that are already serving as altars: sink areas, dressers, desks (home and office), buffets, nightstands and fireplace mantels. These are a few examples of the places you perform daily rituals—both sacred and ordinary.

In my home, I have a hand-whittled dilapidated barn buffet from 1890 that holds a vibrantly colored, jeweled cloth with three favorite books from India, Africa and Morocco stacked together as a foundation for a glowing gold statue of the dancing Shiva. Also on this altar is a railroad key lock housed in rich, hard teak from a railroad line in South Africa that was closed down long ago, along with an equally aged form of a rubber stamp of stars from India. For symmetry and balance, both sides are anchored with dimly lit lamps. This altar consistently reminds me of my passion for the colors of India and for the white lions of South Africa. And Shiva inspires and protects me each time I walk past with devotion.

For me, my bedroom is one large altar. I love to see sacred symbols when I wake up and to go to bed. Surrounded by holy images, I feel a profound sense of joy and protection.

In my bathroom I have another altar. My bathroom's overall energy is African and Moroccan. Buddha shares space on the sink with a white elephant (the divine self), a small offering bowl holds tiny pinecones and pebbled rocks I have found or been given as gifts by dear friends, and a Tibetan box contains my favorite pure essential oils along with my prized possession—a coaster that says "Leap and the net will appear." It is in this grounded, warm sacred space that I prepare for my day or night. Everything I do in this room becomes peaceful and holy.

Spiritual Altars

Traditional altars are any structures where offerings are made for religious or spiritual purposes. Used in many religions, they are frequently located in places of worship, but altars don't just belong in churches. They can be simple and beautiful additions in your home, too.

When deciding where to put an altar, think of its intended purpose. Perhaps it will be used to offer the grace of healing prayer or to manifest something in your life (abundance, for instance). It can also be used simply to acknowledge and celebrate life. The nail salon in my neighborhood has a small altar dedicated to welcoming customers and celebrating the day. It is discreetly placed near the entrance and is neatly arranged: a statue of Buddha, some flowers and a stick of burning incense are balanced by teacups and a small box of donuts, fruit or nuts for customers to enjoy. It's a simple, sweet altar and I always appreciate seeing it. Its offerings keep the intention alive and the welcoming energy flowing.

Practical Altar Intention

Whether we think of them as practical, useful spaces or not, these parts of our homes refresh and calm us. It's easy to lose sight of their sacred aspects. What's most important is that we set them up mindfully as sacred spaces, to allow us to benefit from the time we spend in them. Here's a simple example.

1. Select an organized workspace that feels like it allows life energy flow and efficiency.

2. To keep it balanced, add a green plant or some flowers and arrange a few personal effects that bring you joy.

3. Set your intention: My intention is for this space to be a productive oasis where my creativity thrives.

Spiritual Altar Intention

Forgiveness, for example, is one of the hardest things we as humans can do, so it's a perfect reason to create an altar. Fashion one that uses deities and symbols, and creates a safe and open environment in which to forgive. Write notes to the people who have hurt you. Visit this altar daily and work through letting go of the pain you feel that others have caused you. Keep a green plant or flowers present to keep the energy alive and flowing and to soothe you.

Set your intention: My intention for this spiritual altar is to let my heart release the pain and allow me to forgive those who have hurt me.

Practical Altar

One of the most important things you do, whether or not it's intentional, is choose your habits. Rituals are prayers for order. They sum up who we are as human beings. They define us. They are crucial, because without them we would be distracted and disassociated.

Think of your morning routine as an example. You may snooze once or twice before rising. Hit the shower, where all your lotions, razors, body wash, soaps and shampoos are placed exactly where you left them. Dry off and rush out wearing the robe you left hanging on the same hook yesterday as you will today. Find your articles of clothing in their appropriate drawers and closet space and put them on exactly as you do every other morning. Grab a quick bite to eat. Gather your belongings (and children if you're dropping them off at school). You're not likely to forget that must-have cup of fresh, hot coffee and off you go to the car, bus, subway, bicycle or even the sidewalk. Even our paths to school and work usually follow the same route each day.

Think you're different? Remind yourself of the last time you were in the shower and the shampoo wasn't in its usual place and you had to improvise, or you ran into construction on your way to work and had to quickly find a new route. Ritual broken, that exhale of frustration is your nerves adjusting to the need for immediate change. Life's just like that.

Daily stresses usually don't even stay in our consciousness for more than a few minutes, but they add up over time. All those routines we move in and out of leave most of us longing for downtime. And we seek that downtime in a special place, free from distractions and interruptions. All of us have one of these places, and it is there that we can find examples of practical altars.

Some examples of modern-day practical altars follow in the list below. Some are great centers for hobbies and the necessary upkeep our homes and lives demand. Others are dedicated to creativity and the simple hedonism of having your own space to unwind.

- The well-stocked, well-organized kitchen: Site of those who love to cook, entertain and craft the latest do-it-yourself nutrition.

- The garage: Well-lit and organized, with a workbench or two, the garage is the handyman's holy place.

- Man caves: More than altars, they are shrines to masculinity, with an emphasis on comfort (even castoff furniture is just fine here). Often the site of the best audio and video equipment in the house.

- The dressing room: The shrine to the divine feminine, where women keep (and adorn themselves with) the makeup and cherished jewelry that are part of their regular inner and outer transformations

Practical Altar Intention

Whether we think of them as practical, useful spaces or not, these parts of our homes refresh and calm us. It's easy to lose sight of their sacred aspects. What's most important is that we set them up mindfully as sacred spaces, to allow us to benefit from the time we spend in them. Here's a simple example.

- Select an organized workspace that feels like it allows life energy flow and efficiency.

- To keep it balanced, add a green plant or some flowers and arrange a few personal effects that bring you joy.

- Set your intention: My intention is for this space to be a productive oasis where my creativity thrives.

Outdoor Altars

The exterior parts of our homes have altars, too. We design our landscaping with mulch, stones, solar lights and garden statues. We plant specific flowers in certain ways to achieve themes and patterns, much like a harmonic symphony.

We look forward to spring, when we can be with the earth and touch its "skin" again. We nurture Mother Earth with our love and compassion as the things we tend grow before us. We host parties outside to spend as much time as we can in this life-force energy, made happier because we are thriving in this natural community.

Outdoor Altar Intention

When you choose softscaping elements for your outdoor environment, put some real thought into your selections, as each has its own energetic life force. Give thanks as you place them into the ground. Thank the soil for the nurturing container it will provide for the new plant's roots to grow. Give gratitude to each living species for being part of your sacred space. Have extra gratitude for the seeds or seedlings you choose, because like babies, they need additional love and nurturing.

Set your intention: *My intention for this garden altar is to give thanks to the earth and offer it as sanctuary for her plants and creatures.*

Journaling on Altars

* Where do you participate in your own daily rituals? Where do you pray, dress, read, meditate, fold laundry, exercise, shave, put on makeup, listen to music? (Add any others than occur to you.)

- Where are you guided to place your spiritual altar? Is there a room where you would *not* consider having one?

- Where have you seen beautiful altars that inspire you?

- How comfortable are you letting others see your spiritual side?

Things You Can Do Right Now

1. Introduce flowers or something that you feel is energetically "alive" to your practical or spiritual altar.

2. Make an altar for happiness in the yard or balcony and have it face your home; if you don't have a yard or balcony, find a place for it inside. Place items on it that you are fond of.

3. Set an intention for every practical and spiritual altar in your home.

4. Create a gratitude altar outside for nature and its gifts: bees that make honey, butterflies that represent transformation, gardens that produce food.

Moving on to the Next Chapter

* What energy(s) do you want your altar to hold? Some have a specific reason for being included: new beginnings, motivation, creativity, positive outcomes, the energy of the sun or moon, or abundance. What would your own list be?

* What symbol could you add to your altar that represents peace, love, joy and prosperity for your home?

Another version of an altar is called a spirit house. In Thailand it is believed that the soul doesn't die, so when people pass a temple or spirit house, they raise their hands in prayer to acknowledge those who have already passed on in this lifetime. How does your altar reflect your own spiritual beliefs?

JILL ANGELO

CHAPTER TEN

Solitude

Abide in stillness and you will eventually enter the true way.
                                              — *Tao te Ching*

Solitude is essential, both for creating and appreciating your sacred space. Without a habit of solitude, the crazy business of modern life will take you over and rob you of your soul's peace. I spend most of every day either on my smart phone or attached to my computer (or both). It gets exhausting. While I work in a solitary situation, I definitely do not work in solitude. It isn't until I disconnect—literally "unplug" myself from all that technological energy, close my eyes, come back to center and take one deep cleansing breath—that I fulfill my essential need for peace and solitude.

Think for a moment about what solitude is from a spiritual perspective. It's not about being lonely but rather embracing quiet, celebrating its healing qualities, honoring it as a gift that lets you listen more deeply to your inner world. When you consider solitude in connection with creating your own sacred space, consider these clarifying words and phrases: *calm, stillness, quiet, peace, tranquility.*

Give yourself time for silence. Silence allows for contemplation and reflection. Through silence, we build deeper relationships, both with ourselves and the Divine.

Remember that solitude doesn't require you to close yourself up in your space. One of the world's great writers on the subject of solitude and separation from the grind of life, Henry David Thoreau, chose nature as his place to be alone. Solitude in the sacred space of nature was what clarified his thoughts, fed his soul and gave us the products of his great contemplation. His book Walden is still a masterpiece on the joys of solitude and the deep contemplation it offers to each of us.

Listening as an Art

Solitude introduces you to the art of listening deeply. As you read this chapter, commit yourself to the act and art of being in silence. It is much more than ceasing conversation or turning down the TV; it's not about simply dropping noise to a manageable level. Getting to silence can be a difficult task at first, as we need to listen past the industrial noises that can be almost numbing.

Begin a solitude practice by taking a few minutes to sit outside early in the morning. Take some slow, deep breaths and close your eyes. As your body gets very still, listen.

Listen to the birds. Being able to really hear their song is a new experience for many of us. Then take it a step further and, keeping your eyes closed, listen past them. Can you hear those birds fly? Can you tell what direction they are coming from? Where they are going?

Then move to listening to the wind as it ripples through the grass, trees and flowers.

Next, switch your focus to your own heartbeat. Listen to your breath as you inhale and exhale.

Stretch your solitude practice. Take time to observe when the weather changes or the sun goes down. Sit on the porch and listen to the wind whoosh through the trees, clicking the branches together. Hear the rain as it falls through the air in a rush before it hits the ground. At dusk, listen to the bunny approach in hesitating hops across the lawn.

Listen to the messages your soul gives when you are totally still. It is in this deep reverence for silence that our relationship to the Divine and the great appreciation of sacred space that we are creating moves to a deeper level.

Journaling about Solitude

- Do you crave or avoid solitude?

- What words do you associate with solitude: sad, joyful, lonely, peaceful, boring, frightening, restful, exhilarating? (Add your own.)

- For many of us, the only quiet time we can extract from the day comes during the drive to and from work or the gym—or the part of chauffeuring your children when you have the car to yourself for a few minutes. What are your quiet times and what do you need to do to bring more peace into your day?

Things You Can Do Today

1. How much time per day do you spend in silence? Beginning right now, allow for at least 15 minutes once or twice a day. Then build up daily or weekly for longer periods, until you can give yourself an entire day or weekend in silence. Consider making it a periodic gift to yourself.

2. Drive, run or exercise in silence.

3. We usually spend most of our at-home time in some but not all rooms. Spend a few

minutes in the rooms you visit less often. What do you notice?

4. Take a walk without bringing along any electronics. Be aware of your surroundings. Listen.

5. More ambitious: take a day to unplug from all electronic devices — televisions, computers, music players, tablets and, yes, your cell phone. What energetic changes do you notice? What resistance?

Moving on to the Next Chapter

• How will you commit to more solitude in your life?

• Notice that when you are truly at peace, the objects in your room become more alive. You may get the sense that they want to shift to different locations. What are their messages?

As you begin to practice going into silence, release yourself from the ego-based need to achieve something. Silence and solitude are their own rewards. Keep your breathing centered and focused. Allow a sense of deep peace to spread through your body.

JILL ANGELO

CHAPTER ELEVEN

Purification

Always aim at complete harmony of thought and word and deed. Always aim at purifying your thoughts, and everything will be well.

—Mahatma Gandhi

All of us love a functioning and orderly home, but we are usually so busy living life that keeping things in order simply gets away from us.

The purification stage of creating sacred space is very important. It is a process of evaluating what's in your life and deciding what still has a place and what needs to go. It requires that you pay close attention to all the things that fill your home. Closets and drawers, for instance, are where most of us store our past and present. They represent what we have now and what we have held onto.

We often purchase clothing for the person we think we are—or would like to be. I remember seeing these gorgeous women's tailored shirts with French cuffs and cuff links. They symbolized the money and success of the corporate position I once thought I wanted more than anything. I was thrilled when I bought them. But the truth is, that world and its image weren't what I truly wanted after all. On some level, I knew it. They hung in my closet for years, their very high-priced tags still on them.

The thought of purifying your home and life can feel daunting. That's why when I am working through this stage with clients, we go through their home slowly, evaluating it room by room, breaking the many tasks into bite-sized, manageable pieces. I remind them: spring cleaning isn't just for spring!

Getting Started

Take a moment to do an overview of each room. What is its main purpose, and do the things that currently occupy it serve that purpose? Remove what isn't working for the room's main focus. Look inside baskets, drawers, closets, pantries, cupboards, shelves, under beds—even in your purse, wallet and car. Break all items into three piles:

- What you absolutely want to keep.
- What you no longer need and can give or throw away.
- What you are undecided about.

Take the items you choose to keep, clean as recommended, and locate them to their appropriate places. As for those things that no longer have a place in your life, bless them for their service to you or your home and prepare them to be either given away or disposed of. Blessing is important, because energy travels. You want the things you are sending away to carry good energy with them to the new spaces they will occupy. As for those items you are uncertain about, push yourself to decide again whether they are really worth keeping—or whether it's time for them to move on.

Once this important first step is done, stop for a moment and feel the energy around you shifting. Yes, it will be that fast. The rooms you are changing will be ready for new inspiration.

Letting Go and Moving On

Clothing closets and drawers because they are most often the areas that need to undergo the purification process. As repositories for accumulated, concealed material they can be ignored indefinitely. But now you are making room for the sacred space you are creating. We buy for present or future use, simultaneously creating a past in the process by accumulating more than we need. (When clients follow through with this exercise, nearly everyone is shocked at the amount of clothing they've held onto for sentimental reasons.)

Here are typical examples of clothing that needs to move on and common reasons I have heard for holding onto them.

- Clothes in widely varying sizes because of rollercoaster weight gains and losses.

- Dressy clothing that held special memories from former relationships, despite the fact that both people moved on long ago.

- Clothing that is torn, worn, outdated and has been in need of repair for years and will in truth never be repaired—or worn—again.

- Suits and business wear specific to a profession in which the wearer no longer works.

- Articles purchased for a one-time event or to copy a style seen in a magazine but were never a style the owner liked in the first place.

- Items forgotten about or thought to be lost.

Hanging onto these pieces adds more weight to already burdened psychic fields. Allowing these pieces to be blessed, thanked and passed on through second-hand stores, donated to charity, given to friends or sold removes the energetic bonds to the psyche and can help release the negative feelings attached to them, freeing space for new beginnings on multiple levels.

Energetic Clearing

Once the room has been cleansed of clutter, it is time for energetic cleansing. Following are some of the best methods that have been used for millennia in traditional cultures:

Using smoke and fire

According to an ancient Native American tradition, burning a bundle of white sage (sweet grass, sage, cedar or tobacco) in all four corners of each room removes negativity and energetic blocks. Begin with the side facing north and move clockwise around the room, using circular movements. Circulate the smoke around your aura for the same effect. Pause a moment and be mindful of the shifts occurring. (You can use incense and herbs for cleansing as well.) Light the bundle of sage, then blow it out and circulate the smoke. Dunk it briefly in water to extinguish and, once it has dried out, store it in a cool place.

Candles—use the flame to remove all inner and outer negativity. Set your intention very clearly before lighting, or write out the intention on a piece of paper and burn it to ash in a bowl or fireplace, offering your favorite purifying herbs or tobacco for additional power. Spend time in meditation or prayer with your intention before and after lighting the candle.

Be sure to extinguish any substances you light once you have completed the cleansing. Do not leave candles burning when you leave home or go to bed.

Using sound

As mentioned in chapter four, bells, tingsha cymbals, drums, finger cymbals, crystal drums or Tibetan music bowls are enormously powerful ways to increase the energetic vibrations in your body and in any room.

Set your intention, pause a moment, and use the sound piece in a steady rhythm moving about the room; feel the vibrations grow stronger, clearing blocked energies.

Chakras are energy centers of spiritual power within the human body that help to regulate all its processes, from organ function to the immune system and emotions. There are seven chakras positioned throughout your body, from the base of your spine to the crown of your head. You can imagine chakras as wheels that are rotating.

Opening, cleansing and closing chakras frees stagnant energy. When we keep energy flowing we can prevent blockages from forming. Cleanse your chakra system beginning with the first (root) and moving upward through the torso to the seventh (crown). Pause again and be aware of the shift within you.

Using crystals

Crystals are a gift from the earth and have been proven to emit natural frequencies in harmony with us. This harmony helps balance our inner and outer worlds. Clusters of crystals can clear a room of blocked energy quickly, and can also bring a room back into balance if it is overcharged with energy.

For those of you that use crystals, gather your favorite crystals to create a cluster, or choose specific crystals to cleanse. Display them throughout the room; group them for greater energy if you like. Some clients like to have a form of ritual or ceremony with the crystals, setting intention before placing them in the desired locations.

After you have removed any unwanted items and cleansed the space, set your overall intention for the room. Carefully replace the items you have decided to keep. How do you see them now that the room has been blessed? Seeing them with fresh eyes may lead you to arrange them in new relationships.

Journaling about Purification

- How does energy work in your life?
- How often do you make time to thoroughly clean your home and let go of the things that no longer serve you? Is the cleaning process a therapeutic release or a chore you dread?
- Do you thoroughly cleanse your home only when company is coming over?

Things You Can Do Right Now

1. Light candles more often and do it with intention. (See the gray box for an example.) You can buy candles matched to a specific intention (peace, harmony, abundance, creativity, etc.) or create your own by using the color meanings described in chapter seven.

2. Be mindful about allowing in dark or negative thoughts. Keep positive, clear thoughts throughout your day.

3. Use the greenest or most natural products you can. Doing this serves you, your family

and the environment. (The Naturally Clean Home, by Karyn Siegel-Maier, is loaded with 150 super-easy herbal formulas for green cleaning.)

4. Gather your family together so everyone can be involved in cleaning the whole house in one day, with each member having assigned (or volunteered) responsibilities. Purifying as a group saves time and energy. Play music while you work and make it fun by planning a treat everyone can share once the job is done!

5. Drink eight glasses of water each day to flush impurities out of your system. Make a practice of eating healthy foods.

Moving on to the Next Chapter

* All ancient cultures spent a great deal of time purifying and blessing the home. Decide how you can begin a regular practice of offering an intention to purify and bless your own home.

* What have you learned about the purification process that has surprised you?

An intention is the way you direct conscious purpose or desired outcome to a room. It helps open up the space or area and remove negative, stagnant energy to allow for fresh, positive energy to flow in. Consider the space and the function it provides (bathroom for cleansing, office for clarity or creativity, baby's room for quiet and calm, and so on).

Set the intention (for a bedroom, for example): Bless this room. Let it bring rest, comfort and sanctuary to all who sleep here.

CHAPTER TWELVE

Reading

In the case of good books, the point is not to see how many of them you can get through, but rather how many can get through to you.

—*Mortimer Jerome Adler*

It is astonishing how powerful quotations from a great poet or writer can bring our sacred space to vibrant life.

Each of us has at least one favorite book. Mine is *To Kill a Mockingbird*. I have read it again and again over the years. It feeds my soul and inspires me and my life's purpose. Like all truly good books, it has something new to teach me at whatever age I am when I read it again. In this way it is a never-ending source of wisdom.

In my home, books are a staple of each room's décor. Various titles blend seamlessly with my passion for design, the amazing places I have traveled, and my own spirituality. I place these books in each room to enhance its theme. For example, in my bedroom, I have two ancient poetry books written in Italian, bindings broken, pages torn. One is called Una Passione (One Passion). The other is a series of love letters from a man to his wife. Just having them there brings a perfume of tenderness and excitement and helps create the mystical atmosphere of tantra. (Tantra comes from the Sanskrit word "to weave." Tantra systems are practices that weave together the divine and the "ordinary" in every level.

Two hanging signs make my kitchen sing; one reads, "Nice people rock," and the other "*tshunxeko*," which means "freedom" in the South African dialect of Zulu. I have even spiced up my mud room, which is primarily for my animals, with vinyl stick-ons that say "dog," "woof," "cat," "meow," "roar" and "*tsau*" (the sacred sound that, according to African shamans, accesses the sacred power of lions).

Consider leaving open on a table or kitchen surface one of your favorite books every week at a passage or passages that inspire you. (Be creative and widen your lens. Some of the most enlightening quotes these days come from cookbooks!) Take time to read the passage again and again, so its meanings can become richer for you. You will find that over time the whole atmosphere of your home will become more subtly charged more sacred energy.

Journaling about Reading

- What is your favorite book? Why? How old were you when it made its way to you? Where in your home do you think that book belongs?

* Read your favorite book again and note 10 exhilarating phrases or sentences that remind you why you love the book so much. What do you notice about the book as you reread it? How have the years since you last read it changed the way you look at the world?

* Do you read slowly enough to let the words and meanings really speak to you?

* Do you make time to read for real inspiration?

Things You Can Do Today

1. Decorate your home with books throughout. They are great conversation pieces.

2. Donate or trade in books that you haven't read for new ones.

3. Read a genre you have never tried before.

4. Surround yourself with language: consider the audio version of your favorite book to listen to in the car.

5. Treat yourself to an inspiring moment every day. Read a passage from a daily book of

meditations. (They are widely available in the self-help area of most bookstores.)

6. When you get a new book, pause for a moment before you open it. Marvel at the piece of art it truly is. Consider all that it took to create it.

7. Keep a book in the car with you in case you arrive at your destination early or have to wait.

8. Host a book club.

Moving on to the Next Chapter

* How much time will you commit to dedicate to reading either daily or each week? If you are short on time consider a diurnal, a book with daily meditations, prayers or inspirations. It provides you just enough of a taste to keep you nourished.

* What are your favorite words? Sometimes just painting, writing or cutting them out, placing them on a board and mounting it in a significant location will fill your life with their power. Where will you place them so their messages can continue to inspire you?

Spread your knowledge and joy for reading. Volunteer for a children's session at your local library or help an illiterate adult learn to read.

CHAPTER THIRTEEN

Spiritual Practice

The goal of spiritual practice is full recovery, and the only thing you need to recover from is a fractured sense of self.

—Marianne Williamson

A spiritual practice is a solemn commitment—between you and God, the universe, or a higher power—that you will spend time each day in some form of prayer and/or meditation. Like any regular practice, it works slowly and deeply. Over time, it restores our spirits, helps us build a spiritual foundation of faith and, because it helps awaken our own sense of what the sacred is, it is an essential facet of creating an authentic sacred space.

Spiritual practice aligns with creating sacred space because it puts you in touch with your soul and the divine. Throughout our busy days we hear many "voices" of guidance in response to the choices we make. Often it can be hard to discern what's guiding us—our egos or our souls. When your ego is in charge, the voice will be anxious and pressing, reactionary, a do-this-now type of response. Ego responses can lead to you becoming distracted with "what if?" questions that paralyze you with fear and uncertainty and lead you to make hasty decisions you may later regret. The ego's need to control the situation or outcome is crazy-making, and we can feel the turmoil and anxiety in our bodies.

When the soul is guiding us, the responses are nurturing and calm. This is the quiet, gentle voice we hear and often disregard because, more often than not, the ego is in charge of our response systems. Through spiritual practice, we can begin to discern between the two voices, learning that we cannot control every situation, no matter how hard we try. Rather, we can begin to accept that all is a divinely ordered plan. We have no control, and "surrender" becomes a mantra for us. We start to feel these responses come naturally from our hearts. We have hope, and we learn to trust in something that we cannot see, yet can energetically sense and feel around us.

In order for spiritual practice to be effective, it needs to be daily. Like the rest of the steps in creating a sacred space, make it a ritual and watch the change that comes over you.

How do you build a sacred practice or discipline? Here's how to begin. Make adjustments as time passes.

- First, decide the time of day you feel will be most conducive to doing your practice. Begin by allowing yourself 15 minutes. Choose morning or night.

- Next, make sure there is a space that allows you to be uninterrupted for the time you will need. Use the sacred space set aside for this if you have already set one up.

- Light a candle or burn incense if you wish.

- Read a daily inspiration such as *The Book of Awakening*, by Mark Nepo. Meditate on it. Journal for a few minutes. Mention anything that seems to arise. At the end of your time, say a short closing prayer of thanks.

- Consider drawing from your own religious or spiritual tradition if you have one or grew up with one that still resonates with you.

- If you have dabbled in meditation, consider trying in earnest. If you already meditate, consider how to deepen your practice.

- Listen quietly to nature sounds or other sounds that bring out your connectedness to the universe.

Try this for two weeks and see how it feels. As time goes by and you begin to feel more comfortable with what you are doing, you may want to enrich your daily practice with more sophisticated elements. My dear friend Andrew Harvey, author of *The Hope: A Guide to Sacred Activism*, suggests the following three practices:

- Cool/calm practices keep us calm and grounded. These practices keep us connected to God. Examples: Simple seated meditation, walking meditation, chanting and saying the name of God.

- Warm/fire practices keep the heart center open and flowing with the passion of compassion. They enable the joyful energy of Divine Love to remain alive during times of anger, frustration, anguish and defeat. Examples: Sufi heart practices and Buddhist practices of metta—practicing loving kindness to all beings.

- Sacred body practices keep us conscious of the sacredness of the body. These slowly turn the whole of life into an experience of feast and celebration; every walk, meal, deep sleep or joy at the sight of a flower becomes a form of praise and prayer. Examples: yoga, sacred dance, tai chi or qi gong.

Journaling on Spiritual Practice

* What spiritual practices have you wanted to try?

* When do you feel most connected to the Divine?

* Do you think that since you haven't had a form of spiritual practice before that you are shunned by your god? (Note: that won't happen.)

* How often do you and the Divine communicate? Is it only when you need something (help or stuff)?

* What spiritual crises have come your way that you are grateful for?

* Write down ten blessings in your life and offer a gratitude prayer for them.

Things You Can Do Today

1. Meditate for 15 minutes.

2. Pray for someone you love.

3. Pray for someone with whom you are struggling or having difficulties.

4. Pray for the world.

5. Read a passage from a daily prayer or mediation book.

6. Make time for you and your God—even 15 minutes.

7. Smile at all whose paths you cross.

8. Give back; share your talents.

Moving on to the Next Chapter

* Is your relationship with God outside of the house (church or temple on the weekend or attending an occasional wedding)? How can you welcome God into your house?

* How might having more compassion toward others (and yourself) affect your living environment?

Consider getting out of your comfort zone. Attend a religious service that doesn't reflect your own faith and pay attention to the similarities and differences. Also note any ritual or practices you might want to incorporate into your own spiritual practice.

CHAPTER FOURTEEN

Putting It All Together: Your Space of Grace

There is a candle in your heart, ready to be kindled. There is a void in your soul, ready to be filled. You feel it, don't you?

—*Rumi*

Everything Breathes Together

Sacred space can be a community experience that leads to great intimacy. A wonderful way to include children, for example, is to envision colors, as colors are one of the first components encountered in a space. Ask, "What do you feel when you see this color?" and be amazed at the responses you receive. Children are highly intuitive and oftentimes are not given nearly enough opportunity to share fully.

My husband, a naturally sensitive man, had a conscious idea of what sacred space is. Yet, he tells me again and again being the space I created initially and adding to it with his own spiritual intention has brought peace, joy and deeper understanding of his sacred masculine in relation to my sacred feminine.

If you live with your family or in community, be intentional about balancing your own desires and needs for sacred space with your loved ones'. If space is limited, work together to create a sacred area in the home that is for everyone's use, yet contains personal contributions from each person. Consider a practical altar in the family or great room where all congregate daily.

My Own Space of Grace

As soon as I walked through the front door of my current home, I knew I was going to buy it. Everything about it spoke to me energetically. From the outside, it was the curb appeal and landscaping. On the inside, it was the open floor plan, accented by the intricate crown moldings and natural hardwood floors, as well as the beautifully renovated bath and kitchen. This 101-year-old brick farmhouse would be home to me and my animals, and it would become the focus of what I have been writing about—my sacred space "laboratory."

Having been enthralled by the elements of design for many years, this time I wanted to do things even more consciously. Passionate about the welfare of my animals and the earth, I made the commitment to be environmentally responsible in everything I did. That meant being as green as possible with my decorating, design and lifestyle decisions. I use paint that is environmentally friendly and recycle everything possible. My plants can handle drought, I have a compost pile and I use rain barrels to provide water to my garden and yard. The food I don't grow, I find locally at seasonal farmers markets. I feed my animals the healthiest food I can afford.

I have furnished and designed this home with simple, basic and functional pieces. As I've mentioned, much of what populates my house is from thrift shops, garage sales and scavenger hunts, and is reused purposely to respect my commitment to not overusing. The art pieces I have were either my own creation or carefully chosen. I especially cherish those pieces that come directly from nature, which I consider the source of beauty. Being aged hardwood, the floors are part of that natural feeling as well. While some will disagree with this, I purposely didn't seal my floors because my animals walk and sleep on them daily. Not wanting those chemicals to get into their fur or on the pads of their paws, I clean them with natural cleansers.

As I walk through my home, I see more clearly the person I have become. The interior is built with what remains of my history, grief that resulted in massive change and the willingness to take more risk, special threads that represent celebrated defeats.

Into those celebrated defeats are woven wonderful celebrations that have occurred, too:

welcoming newly rescued four-legged creatures (and seeing the "knowing" each seems to carry of this second chance in their forever home), enjoying the arrival of family and friends for dinner or holiday parties, toasting my decision to take the leap and going into business for myself—and writing this book to share my story and vision. Sacred space helps keep you steady and calm during life's challenges—and all its celebrations.

Every decoration in my home has a story: the guidance and wisdom in the books on the shelves (and how I developed a devotion to their study), the furniture (especially the amazing dilapidated buffet built from the wood of a 120-year-old barn by an artist I met on my way to a flea market), the stones I have collected most of my life, even the colors I chose for my office ("Chocolate" and "Rain"). When I look around my house, I see my own life history, the growth of my own sense of style and an awareness of the many lessons that have graced my life.

This, I believe, is what makes a home sacred. As Anthony Lawlor said, "You enter the temple of home by discovering a new way of seeing, one that reconnects the needs of your soul with the buildings and landscapes that shelter you."

My wish is that you will use this book to rediscover your home's environment and create a sacred space that not only inspires you but also serves as a creative gateway for your spirit.

Now, go have at it and enjoy! And let me know how you're doing. I look forward to hearing from you. Write me at jill@jillangelo.com.

Acknowledgments

If the only prayer you said was thank you, that would be enough.

—Meister Eckhart

Life most definitely is a journey; I have been deeply
To my sweet, loving husband Scott Birnbaum, and to
dear friends Dawn Burton, Colleen Daley, Kathy
Botsford, Lynda Rice and Glenda Gibbs, thank you
for your patience, understanding, flexibility, love,
support and for being incredible cheerleaders of
encouragement—not only during the writing of this
book but every day.

Sincere gratitude to Ellen Gunter and Hollen
Reischer. Their skillful editorial eyes and amazing
journalistic talent were able to take my words,
concepts and thoughts—along with some divine
magic—to create the book you are holding.

Heartfelt gratitude and love to Caroline Myss,
Marianne Williamson and Andrew Harvey. I've felt
honored to be a student of your wisdom, guidance
and teachings, and I feel blessed to call you my
friends.

To my mother Linda, brother Michael, dads Kevin and Tom, and the rest of my incredible family, thank you for supporting the free spirit in me that lives outside of the box and for believing in me, especially during the times when I didn't believe in myself. I love you more than words can say.

And thanks to you, dear reader, for allowing me to be your guide on this journey of creating sacred space. The proceeds from book sales will be used to help, support and care for homeless animals in the Chicagoland area finding forever homes.

Jill Angelo

Brookfield, Illinois

November 2013

Sacred Space

References

BOOKS

These books speak to our inner worlds and the mystical and spiritual journeys we undertake. They are guides to the psyche and the self, great tools for self-care, reading, solitude, spiritual practice and journaling.

Anatomy of the Spirit, by Caroline Myss. The book that opened my life to the richness and mystery of spirituality and changed the way I look at my life.

The Direct Path by Andrew Harvey. How to take a personal journey to the Divine, guided by the world's spiritual traditions.

Everything Belongs by Richard Rohr. A great addition to your meditation space, it speaks of how connected we all are and how significant our thoughts and deeds are.

Illuminata: Thoughts, Prayers, Rites of Passage by Marianne Williamson. An exceptional book of prayers for anyone who would like to speak more personally with the divine.

Earth Calling: A Climate Change Handbook for the 21st Century by Ellen Gunter. About earth consciousness and our commitment to Mother Earth as our physical and spiritual home.

Soul Shaping by Jeff Brown. An invitation to the "School of Heart Knocks," this is a book of inspiration and a guide to finding our more authentic selves.

The Book of Awakening by Mark Nepo. A great source of daily inspiration and a template for spiritual practice.

The following books are references to aid you in creating Sacred Space from an exterior perspective.

The Naturally Clean Home by Karyn Siegel-Maier. The natural (nonchemical) way to clean anything you can think of, with 150 herbal green-cleaning formulas.

The Not So Big House by Sarah Susanka. How to really live in the space you have.

The Simple Home by Sarah Nettleton. The title says it all. The luxury of enough.

Vastu Living, by Kathleen M. Cox. A great introductory book on vastu for Westerners.

Wabi-Sabi for Artists, Designers, Poets and Philosophers by Leonard Koren. My personal favorite on wabi-sabi — simply and tastefully written.

Products

Candles: Candles are sold nearly everywhere now, from high-end department stores to pharmacies (and dozens of online sources). Choose soy-based or beeswax candles; they are the most natural and least polluting. (Paraffin candles are the most polluting.) Try mine if you like (www.jillangelo.com)!

Incense: www.shoyeido.com
My favorite choice from this site is Japanese incense.

Sweetgrass and Sage: www.taosherb.com
Great source for the materials you need to clear the energy in
your home. Another word for clearing energy is "smudging."

Young Living Essential Oils: www.youngliving.com
Great source for therapeutic-grade essential oils.

KION YAMAGUCHI PRESS

IMPRINT OF TAYEN LANE

SAN FRANCISCO

MONTREAL

WWW.TAYENLANE.COM

Sacred Space

JILL ANGELO

CPSIA information can be obtained at www.ICGtesting.com
Printed in the USA
LVOW11s1519100316

478624LV00002B/479/P